Don't Have A Messed-Up Sunday School Or Church School

Don't Have A Messed-Up Sunday School Or Church School

A BOOK TO HELP ORGANIZE YOUR SUNDAY SCHOOL OR CHURCH SCHOOL

DR. ONEAL C. SANDIDGE

AuthorHouse™
1663 Liberty Drive
Bloomington, IN 47403
www.authorhouse.com
Phone: 1-800-839-8640

Published by AuthorHouse   08/10/2012

ISBN: 978-1-4107-5229-1 (sc)
ISBN: 978-1-4107-5228-4 (e)

Library of Congress Control Number: 2003093083

Printed in the United States of America

OTHER BOOKS BY ONEAL SANDIDGE

Four books were originally published on a national label-Sunday School Publishing Board, Nashville, Tennessee

- ➤ *I'M STUCK!—HELP ME START A YOUTH MINISTRY IN THE AFRICAN-AMERICAN CHURCH*

- ➤ *TEACHER TRAINING IN THE AFRICAN-AMERICAN CHURCH*

- ➤ *STRATEGIES FOR THE DIRECTOR OF CHRISTIAN EDUCATION*

- ➤ *BEYOND THE CLASSROOM*

- ➤ *A BOOK TO CHANGE YOUR LIFE: THE PASTOR'S LIFE, CHURCH LIFE, AND CHURCH LEADERSHIP ABOUT MINSITRY*

SCRIPTURE AND VERSION

All Scripture is taken from the **King James Version** of the Bible or New Revised Standard Version of the Bible

DEDICATION

- **God be the Glory**
- **My Pastor: Scottie Craft**
- **My Mother: Hattie Dawson Sandidge**
- **My Father: The late Wardie Sandidge**
- **My Wife's Mother and Father-The late Joseph Oliver and Mable Gilmore Oliver**
- **My Wife: Janice Oliver**
- **Sister: Arlean S. Hunter**
- **Sister-in-laws: Evangelist Barbara Slaughter and Gloria Oliver**
- **Brother-in laws: Bishop David Slaughter and William (Billy) Oliver**
- **Nephews and nieces: Joseph (Joey)Oliver, Rodney Oliver, William K. Hunter, Jr., Azell Slaughter, and Larry D. Hunter, Talitha Slaughter, and Kimberly Oliver**
- **Our children: Jermaine Sandidge and Ieke Sandidge**
- **Our grandchildren: Amea Harvey, Akeria Harvey, Alyssa Barrett, and Mekhi Sandidge**
- **Our godson and wife, Rev. Ronnie Clark and Tonia Clark**
- **My assistant's mother: Wilma Baskerville and children: Lea Baskerville and Gerald Baskerville**
- **Mr. William H. Ware IV and mother, Mrs. Deborah C. Ware**
- **Provided multiple ways of assistance: Deacon Grady Davis and Deaconess Betty Davis**
- **Friends unforgettable since high school: Gary Mays and Wanda Mays**
- **My assistant and godson: Eric M. Baskerville, Sr. and god-grand son, Eric Maurice Baskerville, Jr.**
- **Aunts and Uncles living: Cammie Miller, Dorothy Jones, Sally Dawson, and Robert Dawson**
- **Cousins: Ernest Haynes, Deborah Harris, Linda Dawson, Charlie Waugh, and Jackie Ponder, Sarah D. Stevenson.**

ACKNOWLEDGMENTS

Mr. Eric Baskerville Richmond, Virginia
Assistant, Typist, and Reader

Antoinette Vallrie and Janice Oliver Sandidge,
Readers

Convent Avenue Baptist Church, a mega church New York City where Patricia Spence, a most dedicated Superintendent worked with Dr. Oneal Sandidge as Director of Education. Dr. Sandidge's knowledge in Christian education led him to develop this book from an experience-based position.

SPECIAL THANKS FOR INTERVIEWS

- Mr. William H. Ware, IV
- Mr. Eric M. Baskerville, Sr.
- Mrs. Janice Sandidge

SPECIAL THANKS FOR FOREWORD

- Ms. Antoinette Vallrie

SPECIAL THANKS FOR AFTERWORD 2004

- Mr. Eric M. Baskerville, Sr.

SPECIAL THANKS FOR AFTERWORD 2012

- Mr. William H. Ware, IV

SPECIAL THANKS FOR PHOTOS

- Janice O. Sandidge
- Eric M. Baskerville, Sr. and Stephanie Watts, Parents of Eric M. Baskerville, Jr.
- Stephanie Watts, Parent of Devin Watts
- William H. Ware, IV
- Ieke Sandidge
- Jermaine Sandidge and Myesha Johnson, Parents of Makhi Sandidge
- Keshoun Littles, Sr. and Lea Baskerville, Parents of Keshoun Littles, Jr.
- Sidney Miller and Ethel Miller, Parents of Devine Miller

CONTENTS

FOREWORD

Ms. Antoinette H. Vallrie, M.S.

Assuredly, it can be stated that the church school or Sunday school has long been the teaching cornerstone of the Baptist church. Nearly every Christian can recall that he or she learned some profound, life-changing Biblical truth while attending Sunday school. For these reasons, it is imperative that we continue to strive for excellence in the Christian classroom, further equipping the saint for Kingdom-building work.

Don't Have a Messed up Sunday School or Church School is unmatched in its clarity and direction which qualifies it to be a credible resource for Christian educators. The thorough and detailed handiwork of Dr. Oneal Sandidge makes him a standout among his colleagues and other notable figures in the field of Christian education. He takes a reader on a journey through historical and traditional venues, as well as contemporary and innovative research. He answers all questions and has "left no stone unturned" in his efforts to address concerns of those who are involved in, and perhaps are struggling with organizing a church school.

Most impressive are the job applications and job descriptions of the church school. Dr. Sandidge ushers in a climate of professionalism that is rare in our congregations. The DCE and staff have the awesome privilege of making volunteers feel like Christian educators and not just "youth workers" or "Sunday school helpers." With this structure, everyone involved is valued and respected for whatever contributions they extend.

Consequently, *Don't Have a Messed up Sunday School or Church School* is remarkably personal in nature. As the Christian educator digests the wealth of knowledge laid before him, he or she can sense the passion and sincerity of Dr. Sandidge, who targets every facet of church school ministry, highlighting current trends and organizational designs. He is empathetic in understanding the anxieties of Christian educators. It is so refreshing to note that he sees the need for teacher retreats and fellowships—a must to avoid spiritual burnout. Not only are years of experience reflected in this guidebook, but it is laden with scripture references to support the notion that the church school does not operate by theory or opinion, but that the fundamental basis is God's Holy and Divine Word.

Additionally, through the spiritual hierarchy set forth in this book, the Christian educator is held accountable not only to God and co-laborers, but to those students that God has placed in the classroom. Dr. Sandidge challenges the Christian educator to become more intentional in preparation and follow-up procedures. For further emphasis, Dr. Sandidge has given the Christian educator a virtual blueprint on how to conduct meetings and how to navigate opportunities for dialogue and affirmation within the church school. His clear, easily readable visual aids and self-evaluations are essential for ongoing modifications.

Finally, ***Don't Have a Messed up Sunday School or Church School*** has a mission, a purpose, and a vision undergirded by the Bible through the Holy Spirit with the life of Christ as the ultimate model. From this plethora of ideas and methodology, the Christian educator can sense Dr. Sandidge's heart that is reflective of an inner conviction for God's people, His purposes, and His divine plans.

It is my prayer that African American churches would be compelled to raise the standard in leadership, teaching, evangelism, and mentoring. Whether your church school is firmly established or is in need of a "spiritual renovation", I am confident that the aforementioned attributes make ***Don't Have a Messed up Sunday School or Church School*** a worthy and invaluable tool for all Christian educators who desire to "walk worthy of their calling."

Ms. Antoinette H. Vallrie, M.S.

Currently: Youth minister and Sunday School Teacher

Former: Public School Teacher

Degrees: B.A. English Education—McNeese State University, Lake Charles, LA M. Ed—Administration and Supervision Southern University Baton Rouge, LA and M.DIV. Southern Baptist Theological Seminary

DON'T HAVE A MESSED-UP SUNDAY SCHOOL OR CHURCH SCHOOL—A BOOK TO HELP ORGANIZE YOUR SUNDAY SCHOOL OR CHURCH SCHOOL

Never Forget the Foundation of the Church School: The Church

INTRODUCTION

Take a moment to reflect to your Sunday school blueprint. How long has it been since your Sunday school or church school has been evaluated? What ratings did the superintendent, assistant superintendents, teachers, workers, and students receive? What about the organization of the school? How is the school organized? Do leaders and teachers know their roles and duties? Do teachers and support staff understand their titles, the reasons for teachers, the required work to be an effective teacher, and perhaps what teachers should or should not do? Maybe some churches find themselves with a messed up Sunday school or church school, a school where there seems to be few organizational skills. **This handbook will assist leaders to rethink ideas for organizing or reorganizing a Sunday school or church school.**

WHAT IS A SUNDAY SCHOOL OR CHURCH SCHOOL HANDBOOK?

A Sunday school or church school handbook allows teachers, leaders, a support team (workers), and students to understand the operation of the Sunday school or church school. It sets calmness to frustration caused by misinterpretation, misunderstanding, and perhaps, poor communication. A handbook serves as a **doorknob for visitors**. It also serves as an **order for leaders**, teachers, the support team, and students. Visitors can turn the knob that directs them in the right spiritual, educational direction. Climaxing is a framework of "knowingality" for everyone.

A Sunday school or church school handbook is an order established by leaders of the Sunday school or church school, recommended by the superintendent, and reviewed and approved by a director of Christian education or a pastor. (Usually the pastor approves plans in the absence of the director of Christian education. In any case, the pastor should review the handbook.) **The handbook provides answers to questions related to program administration**. The handbook may be developed into Sunday school or church school mini handbooks, especially sections about prospective teachers and current teachers. The handbook is a component of the Department of Christian Education Handbook. **This book is derived from real experiences per teaching college and graduate students Christian education for many years, serving in university/college administration, and working in mega churches as leader in Christian education. What is a messed-up Sunday church school?**

A messed up Sunday or church school is when the church school or what some call Sunday school, is not smoothly operating, disjointed, unclear directions, and sometimes just "lost". A messed up church school is also

when any person or group does not understand the goals, objectives, and ways of church school administration. The church school is further messed up when other ministries and church schools are not working as a unit to provide ministry. *This book discusses this one day school, for an hour or so, whether it meets on Saturdays, Sundays, or another day.*

A school that teaches academics, i.e., a Christian school, grades Pre-K, or K through elementary or perhaps high school, is not my focus. **My focus is upon a school where teachers volunteer and use a Sunday school or church school book and perhaps only the Bible for religious instruction.** This focus is on any school that causes students to indulge in some type of Biblical study beyond the sermon, regular Bible-study, and prayer services.

This book is one of many to help church leaders organize or reorganize the church school. Help is provided to assist pastors, church teachers, Professors of Christian Education, Directors of Christian education, church school superintendents, the support team, and students to reevaluate the Sunday school or church school. **The key to developing a holistic Sunday school or church school is to discuss the operation of the Sunday school or church school. Every Sunday school or church school needs order, direction, instruction, and clear understanding of procedures, operations, and other administrative icons.** *A Sunday school or church school handbook is the most practical solution to a messed up Sunday school or church school.*

Terms in this book: "church school" means the same as "Sunday school." A Sunday school operates on Sunday and a church school operates on another day to fulfill the requirements met in Sunday school. An academic church school differs because academic instruction takes place daily, and usually, employees are salaried. The terms "Support Staff" and "Support Team" refer to workers who assist leaders and teachers.

This book will suggest ways to develop or modify a church school. **Chapter one** provides some steps for developing a church school handbook, **chapter two** provides forms that the church school may consider for use for modifying a church school, **chapter three** addresses current teachers, **chapter four** addresses prospective teachers, **chapter five** alludes to the support team, **chapter six** provides a message to superintendents, and **chapter seven** concludes with a discussion about the future of Sunday schools or church schools and also includes two interviews.

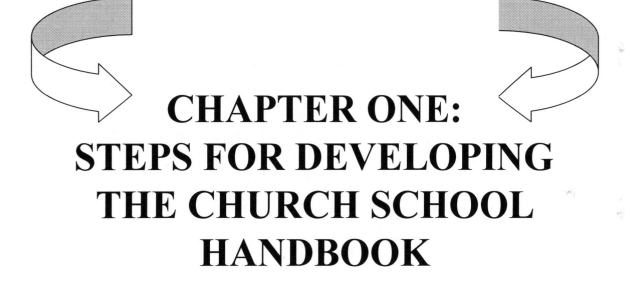

CHAPTER ONE:
STEPS FOR DEVELOPING
THE CHURCH SCHOOL
HANDBOOK

CHAPTER ONE:
STEPS FOR DEVELOPING THE CHURCH
SCHOOL HANDBOOK

The church school handbook should be developed through much care, prayer, and spiritual enlightenment. This handbook will provide on-hand information for visitors and church members. The superintendent, the person responsible for this ministry, must carefully decide what to do first. This chapter will provide suggestions for the superintendent to consider when developing the handbook.

The superintendent must keep in mind that the Sunday or church school's **main purpose is to provide Christian instruction**. Matthew 28:20 reminds us:

Teaching them to observe all things whatsoever I have commanded you: and, lo, I am with you always, even unto the end of the world. Amen

Leaders are reminded to teach. In turn, those taught, will hopefully become teachers. 2 Timothy 2:2 reminds us about responsibilities:

And the things that thou hast heard of me among many witnesses, the same commit thou to faithful men, who shall be able to teach others also.

Ephesians 4:11-12 also reminds the pastor and teacher of responsibilities:

And he gave some, apostles; and some, prophets; and some, evangelists; and some, pastors and teachers; for the perfecting of the saints for the work of the ministry, for the edifying of the body of Christ:

The total church program is also biblical. Acts 2:42-47 informs us about instruction, worship, fellowship, and instruction. The scripture verses read:

And they continued steadfastly in the apostles' doctrine and fellowship, and in breaking of bread, and in prayers. And fear came upon every soul: and many wonders and signs were done by the apostles. And all that believed were together, and had all things common; and sold their possessions and goods, and parted them to all men, as every man need. And they, continuing daily with one accord in the temple, and breaking bread from house to house, did eat their meat with gladness and singleness of heart, Praising God, and having favour with all the people. And the Lord added to the church daily such as should be saved.

The Old Testament gives an example where everybody received instruction.

Deuteronomy 31:12 reads:
Gather the people together, men, and women, and children, and thy stranger that is within thy gates, that they may hear, and that they may learn, and fear the LORD your God, and observe to do all the words of this law:

Children

Ephesians 6:4:
And, ye fathers provoke not your children to wrath: but bring them up in the nurture and admonition of the Lord.

Home Bible Studies

Acts 2:46:
And they, continuing daily with one accord in the temple, and breaking bread from house to house, did eat their meat with gladness and singleness of heart,

Acts 5:42:
And daily in the temple, and in every house, they ceased not to teach and preach Jesus Christ.

Time frame: It usually takes **four to six** months to develop a handbook.

The **superintendent**, usually assisted by **assistant superintendent(s),** decides on headings for the handbook. The **superintendent** suggests names of persons that could be used in sections of the handbook. Depending on the size of the church school, one person may be given more than one assignment.

Compilers should report suggestions within one month from the assignment date. The superintendent may modify plans, if needed, and provide a rough draft to two or three blind readers. **Blind readers** should have one month to review and make suggestions. The superintendent should prepare a final draft for pastor or the director of Christian education, requesting suggestions. It is important to suggest a one-month deadline for review. It is also wise to state that "no response" mean "no suggestion." The superintendent can revise and place a final copy in binder form, save two or more disks for filing, give a disk to each leader, and print a small booklet for members. Professional printing is recommended.

The superintendent is responsible for what goes on in the church school. He or she should carefully rethink the organizational structure of the school.

The Organization

The organization plan of the Sunday school or church school should:

➢ recognize God and teach Godly principles
➢ be flexible
➢ be reasonable
➢ cause people to relate to real-life issues
➢ relate to church focus and complement other ministries
➢ be easy to follow
➢ be shared by all
➢ be open for revision

The Sunday school or church school must recognize that **Christian education** is **needed** because of **edification** (Matthew 28:20), because of **evangelism** (Matthew 28:19), and to help Christians **spiritually grow.**

Steps one to three are suggestions to assist the superintendent in developing a handbook.

STEP ONE: A SUPERINTENDENT SHOULD REFINE SKILLS TO OPERATE A CHURCH SCHOOL

Purpose: This major teaching department is responsible for teaching all parishioners. A superintendent must hear, listen, and seek help to organize or reorganize a church school. The superintendent may need additional training to empty the best skills, i.e. communication skills, how to handle conflict, and how to respond to concerns as a Christian.

STEP TWO: THE SUPERINTENDENT IS RESPONSIBLE FOR THE FINAL ORGANIZATION OF THE SCHOOL HANDBOOK

Purpose: The church school superintendent, after approval by pastor or director of Christian education, recommends the handbook to the church. The superintendent, in conjunction with director of Christian education or pastor, is responsible for handbook **content.**

SUGGESTED HANDBOOK CONTENT STEPS

The content often includes the following:

♦ handbook compilation committee
♦ the church's mission statement
♦ the pastor's mission statement
♦ church school mission statement
♦ school's history
♦ goals for the school and goals for each department (all grades)
♦ objectives for the school and objectives for each department (all grades)
♦ theme
♦ flow charts: the church; the department of Christian education, and the Sunday school
♦ an administrative calendar—meeting dates and events for the school
♦ job descriptions
   a) superintendent
   b) assistant superintendents
   c) church school support staff
      1. librarian and assistant librarian
      2. vacation Bible school coordinator program
      3. assistants and others
   d) administrator for prospective teacher and current teacher training
   g) the elective course offering administrator
   h) teachers
♦ hours of school operation
♦ design of classes
♦ collecting offering procedure
♦ agenda for superintendents
♦ discipline policies for
   a) administrators
   b) teachers
   c) students
   d) support team
♦ how to request information

- financial procedures, including how to make requests for funds
- school dress code
- curriculum review and curriculum materials: dates and procedures
- the Bible version for each grade
- purchasing materials for teaching
- using supplementary materials
- opening school day order
- end of the school year closing day order
- promotional exercises bulletin
- confidential records and folders for students and staff
- missed class assignments for students and staff
- attendance and substitute teacher's policies
- evangelism guidelines
- mentoring guidelines
- retreats
- field trip permission slips
- emergencies
- lesson overview
- sample evaluations for church school: school, teachers, students, leaders, and support team
- open house day
- special missions project day
- church statistician
- sample meeting agenda for
  a) superintendent
  b) church school
- sample meeting agenda for
  a) director of Christian education
  b) superintendent
- sample meeting agenda for
  a) superintendent
  b) teachers
  c) support team
- other suggested sample meeting agenda for
  a) teachers
  b) support team
- classes/grades or ages for instruction
- length of service agreement
- bulletin board chair
- teacher training administrator

♦ internship for prospective teachers
♦ special fun night

The superintendent may get other leaders to assist with plans.

STEP THREE: PURPOSE FOR HANDBOOK CONTENT STEPS

• **The Church's Mission Statement**

Purpose: The purpose is to remind the church school about the direction the church is headed. The first chapter of the handbook may include the church's Mission Statement. Contact the director of Christian education or the pastor for this statement. In some cases, the superintendent may need to recommend that the church prepares this statement.

• **The Pastor's Mission Statement**

Purpose: The church school needs to understand the direction the pastor is headed. The first chapter of the handbook may include the pastor's Mission Statement. In some cases, the superintendent may need to recommend that the church prepares this statement.

• **The Church School Mission Statement**

Purpose: Every school needs to decide where they are headed. The church school should develop the school's mission statement by incorporating the church and pastor's mission statements in a teaching tone but not extracting meaning from the church or pastor's Mission Statements.

• **Select a Team to Suggest Goals and Objectives**

Purpose: This list guides the church school to have a focus and direction. The Mission Statement, goals, objectives, and school themes should be developed for three years. Three years provide time for long-term planning. The superintendent may ask for suggestions but the superintendent recommends the final submission.

• **School Themes**

Purpose: The school should have an annual theme that focuses on church needs.

- **The Superintendent and Director of Christian Education Should Include Flow Charts**

Purpose: The superintendent should use the church flow chart and the Christian education flow chart to create a church school flow chart which shows "order of command" of the school. All charts should be a part of the handbook.

- **General Superintendent and Assistant Superintendent May Develop an Annual Calendar for the School**

Purpose: The calendar of all events should be noted. A calendar helps leaders, school teachers, workers, and students to know what lies ahead.

The **calendar** may include, but not limited to:

- ☐ **current teacher training dates**
- ☐ **new teacher training dates**
- ☐ **dates for teacher retreats**
- ☐ **school's opening and closing dates**
- ☐ **promotional exercise date**
- ☐ **church school picnic date**
- ☐ **church school fun nights dates (two during the year)**
- ☐ **due dates for lesson plans**
- ☐ **dates for leaders to meet**
- ☐ **dates for teacher meetings**
- ☐ **prospective teacher internship dates**
- ☐ **dates for school evangelism**
- ☐ **other suggested dates.**

(See Appendices in Dr. Sandidge's **STRATEGIES FOR THE DCE**.)

- **Job Descriptions**

Purpose: Descriptions will help each person to learn his or her responsibilities for the assignment.

- **Hours of School Operation**

Purpose: Students, teachers, leaders, the congregation, and visitors need to know hours of operation.

- **Design of Classes**

Purpose: The entire school should be able to glance at how classes are designed: age groups or by grades.

- **Collecting Offering Procedure**

Purpose: The entire school needs to know how and when offerings are collected.

- **Agenda For Superintendents**

Purpose: All superintendents should have a general idea of meeting agendas. Certain elements will remain the same for all meetings.

- **Superintendent Decides on Disciplinary Action Policies**

Purpose: To decide how class discipline will be handled.

- **How to Request Information**

Purpose: The entire school needs to know the protocol and procedure for requesting information.

- **Financial Procedures**

Purpose: Every staff person needs to understand how financial procedures are handled.

- **Superintendent Decides on Dress Code**

Purpose: To decide how leaders, teachers, students, and workers will dress when attending classes and events.

- **Entire School Staff Decides on Curriculum Review**

Purpose: To make suggestions for improving course content: the text (literature from publisher or elsewhere), special classes: dates, instructors, time for such classes, topics, subjects, or themes that relate to Mission Statement.

- **The Superintendent Decides on Bible Version for Teachers and Students** (Consult pastor or Director of Christian education.)

Purpose: To elect the required Bible versions for all teachers and students. Different Bible versions may be elected for children, youth, and perhaps young adults.

- **Purchasing Material for Teaching**

Purpose: All staff should know limitations and requests and procedures for purchasing teaching materials.

- **Using Supplementary Materials**

Purpose: Each staff person should be informed about incorporating supplementary materials.

- **Opening School Day Order**

Purpose: The first day of each school year should be discussed.

- **End of the School Year Closing Day Order**

Purpose: The last day of each school year should be discussed.

- **Superintendent or Assistant Superintendent(s) Decides on Promotional Exercises**

Purpose: To allow students to learn according to grades or ages.

- **Confidential Records and Folders for Students and Staff**

Purpose: The staff and students should be informed why records and folders are confidential and where they are stored.

- **Missed Class Assignments for Students**

Purpose: Students should be informed about missed class assignments.

- **Superintendent Decides on Attendance and Substitutes Policies**

Purpose: To discuss absences for teachers, workers, and students. To determine how many absences are allowed, the consequences, who to call to report absences, and how or who to contact substitutes.
(Suggestion: Use the list of trained prospective teachers)

- **Superintendent or Assistant Superintendent Decides on Evangelism Guidelines**

Purpose: To decide how Evangelism will be incorporated into the church school program.—To elect an Evangelism Chair, decide on training for the chair, and to decide how often the church school Evangelism Team should meet.—The actual steps for evangelism may be shared.

- **Superintendent or Assistant Superintendent Decides on Mentoring Guidelines**

Purpose: To discuss and develop application for mentoring and mentors.

- **Entire School Staff Decides on Retreats**

Purpose: To decide on the goals and objectives, content, program, and retreat order for the next two retreats. Note: A retreat is to refresh staff, not to teach.

- **Entire School Decides on Field Trip Permission Letter**

Purpose: To develop or revise permission slips and non-liability for students under age 18.

- **Emergencies**

Purpose: Personal emergencies: family phone calls, on-site emergencies, physical, and fire drill procedures should be discussed.

- **Lesson Overview**

Purpose: To define the purpose, review scriptures, and to provide a brief summary.

- **Sample Evaluations for Church School: School, Students, Teachers, Leaders, and Support Team**

Purpose: Students, the program, and workers should be evaluated at some point.

- **Open House Day**

Purpose: The school should consider a day to share with the congregation and community the course offerings and staff.

- **Special Missions Project Day**

Purpose: The church school should consider a special missions project.

- **Church Statistician**

Purpose: The school needs a person to serve as auditor for financial bookkeeping.

- **Sample Meeting Agenda for General Superintendent and Church School**

Purpose: The general superintendent should be provided the DCE meeting agenda.

- **Sample Meeting Agenda For DCE and General Superintendent**

Purpose: The general superintendent should have an idea of the meeting agenda with the DCE.

- **The Superintendent Decides on the Lesson Plan Requirements for Teachers**

Purpose: To learn what will be taught in classes. The type of plan, how often plans are due, who to turn in plans to, and locations for collecting plans are important.

The Superintendent or Appointed Person(s) Develops:

- **The Superintendent Selects a Committee to Develop the School History**

Purpose: To interview present church leaders, church members, previous and present church school leaders, students, and pastor.

- **A Superintendent Elects a Team to Suggest Classes/Grades or Ages for Instruction**

Purpose: To determine classes or grades and ages of students for placement and room assignments.

Questions include:

What will the program look like? Where will the occasion take place? What kinds of decorations for the event are needed? Who will speak for the event? Where will students go next? At what grade or age will promotions end? How will students be promoted?

(Suggestion: Promotion ends after young adult class for most schools.) *Decide on graduation program and all details.* (See Appendices in Dr. Sandidge's **STRATEGIES FOR THE DCE**.)

- **Superintendent Decides on Length of Service Agreement**

Purpose: To decide how long school leaders, teachers, and workers should serve.

- **Superintendent Elects a Handbook Compilation Committee**

Purpose: To decide the order for compiling a handbook and deadlines.

- **Superintendent Decides on Bulletin Board Chair**

Purpose: To decide on dates for new boards: classrooms, hallways, events, and announcements.

- **Elect a Prospective Teacher Training and a Current Teacher Training Program Administrator**

Purpose: To suggest teacher training programs and calendar dates for prospective teachers and current church teachers. (What teachers should know, decide on an application for instructors, when and how instructors will be selected, to determine who makes final decisions, and to require a course syllabus from selected instructors) (See Appendices in Dr. Oneal Sandidge's **STRATEGIES FOR THE DCE**.) The administrator also develops evaluations for current and prospective teachers, provides the internship application, and maintains completed evaluations.

The Internship for Prospective Teachers

Purpose: To decide on internship dates

(Suggestion: two months) and duties for teachers serving as supervised teachers for prospective teachers (See Appendices in **STRATEGIES FOR THE DCE**.)

Entire School Staff and Students Decide on Special Fun Nights

Purpose: To decide on dates and fun activities for the next three years—To decide who will be responsible for planning and preparing the agenda for fun night. This may take place once or twice a year.

STEP FOUR: ADHERE TO SUGGESTIONS FROM PASTOR AND THE DIRECTOR OF CHRISTIAN EDUCATION

STEP FIVE: ATTEND WORKSHOP TRAINING SESSION TO UPDATE SKILLS.

Plans for Developing Our Handbook

Plans for Developing Our Handbook

Plans for Developing Our Handbook

Plans for Developing Our Handbook

Plans for Developing Our Handbook

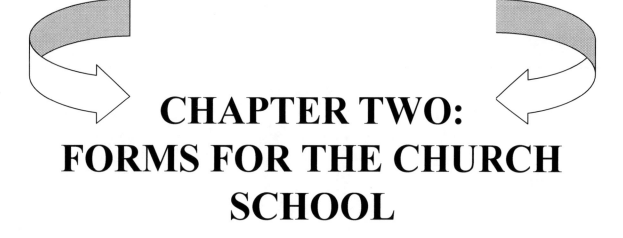

CHAPTER TWO:
FORMS FOR THE CHURCH
SCHOOL

CHAPTER TWO:
FORMS FOR THE CHURCH SCHOOL

This chapter is similar to an appendix, except this chapter goes beyond appendices. These forms are examples for a church school to consider when modifying or organizing a church school. The following sample forms will assist one to develop forms for the handbook.

- Form A : Mission Statement
- Form B : Goals
- Form C : Objectives
- Form D : The Flow Chart
- Form E : An Administrative Calendar
- Form F : Job Descriptions

1F: Superintendent

2F: Assistant Superintendents

3F: Support Team

    3F-1: Department Secretaries

    3F-2: Class Secretaries and Assistant Secretaries

    3F-3: Librarian and Assistant Librarian

    3F-4: Vacation Bible School Coordinator

    3F-5: Program Administrator for Prospective Teacher Training and Current Teacher Training

    3F-6: The Elective Course Offering Administrator

- Form G : Hours of School Operation
- Form H : Design of Classes
- Form I : Collecting Offering
- Form J : An Agenda for Superintendents
- Form K : Discipline Policies for Administrators, Teachers, and Students
- Form L : Request Information
- Form M : Learn Financial Procedures
- Form N : Dress Code for School
- Form O : Curriculum Review and Curriculum Materials
- Form P : The Bible Version
- Form Q : Purchasing Materials
- Form R : Using Supplementary Materials
- Form S : Opening School Day

- Form T : End of the School Year Closing Day
- Form U : Promotional Exercises
- Form V : Confidential Records and Folders
- Form W : Missed Class Assignments
- Form X : Attendance and Substitutes Policies
- Form Y : Evangelism Guidelines
- Form Z : Mentoring Guidelines
- Form AA : Retreats
- Form BB : Field Trip Permission Slips
- Form CC : Emergencies
- Form DD : Lesson Overview
- Form EE : Sample Evaluations for Church School Leaders
- Form FF : Open House Day
- Form GG : Special Missions Project Day
- Form HH : Church Statistician
- Form II : Sample Meeting Agenda for Superintendent and Church School
- Form JJ : Sample Meeting Agenda for Director of Christian Education and Superintendent
- Form KK : Sample Meeting Agenda for Superintendent, Teachers, and Support Team
- Form LL : Other Suggested Sample Meeting Agendas with Teachers and Support Team

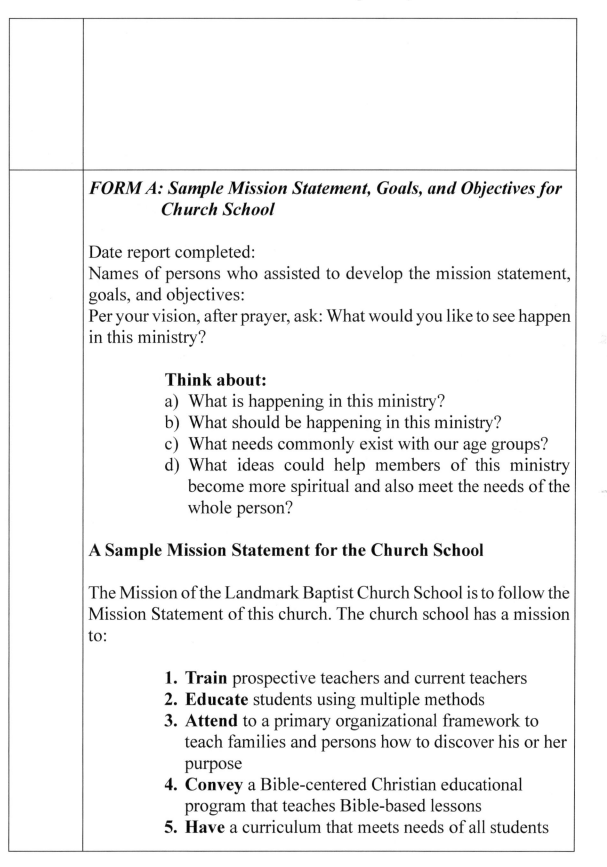

FORM A: Sample Mission Statement, Goals, and Objectives for Church School

Date report completed:

Names of persons who assisted to develop the mission statement, goals, and objectives:

Per your vision, after prayer, ask: What would you like to see happen in this ministry?

Think about:
a) What is happening in this ministry?
b) What should be happening in this ministry?
c) What needs commonly exist with our age groups?
d) What ideas could help members of this ministry become more spiritual and also meet the needs of the whole person?

A Sample Mission Statement for the Church School

The Mission of the Landmark Baptist Church School is to follow the Mission Statement of this church. The church school has a mission to:

1. **Train** prospective teachers and current teachers
2. **Educate** students using multiple methods
3. **Attend** to a primary organizational framework to teach families and persons how to discover his or her purpose
4. **Convey** a Bible-centered Christian educational program that teaches Bible-based lessons
5. **Have** a curriculum that meets needs of all students

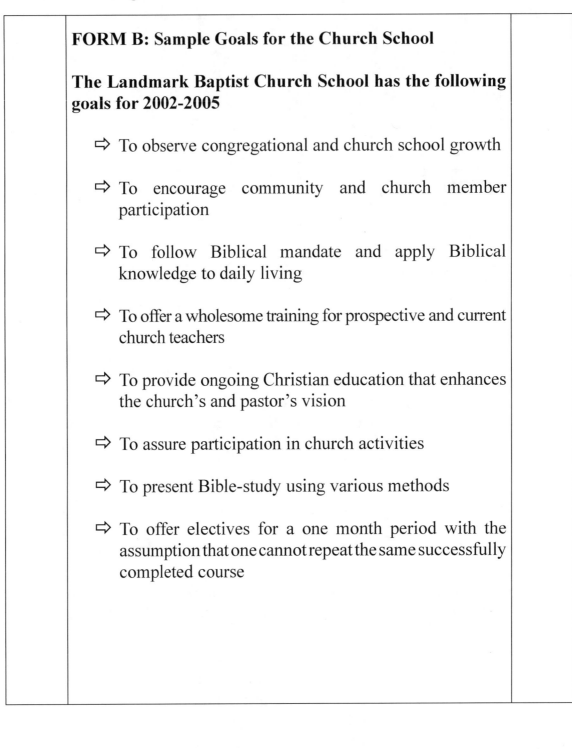

FORM B: Sample Goals for the Church School

The Landmark Baptist Church School has the following goals for 2002-2005

⇨ To observe congregational and church school growth

⇨ To encourage community and church member participation

⇨ To follow Biblical mandate and apply Biblical knowledge to daily living

⇨ To offer a wholesome training for prospective and current church teachers

⇨ To provide ongoing Christian education that enhances the church's and pastor's vision

⇨ To assure participation in church activities

⇨ To present Bible-study using various methods

⇨ To offer electives for a one month period with the assumption that one cannot repeat the same successfully completed course

FORM C: Sample Objectives for the Church School

The Landmark Baptist Church School agrees on the following objectives for the church school, 2002-2005.

The church school will educate students to:

○ **govern** themselves and learn the mandate of pastor, church, and church leaders

○ **use** the Bible to increase Biblical knowledge in order to have a more productive spiritual lifestyle

○ **identify** personal goals that will lead to discovering and exercising "purpose for living"

○ **direct** others to Christ

○ **enter** and obtain church membership and church school information

---

FORM D: A Sample Flow Chart for the Church

The church should have a flow chart that shows the hierarchy of leadership positions. The church school should also have a flow chart. This flow chart may be developed in conjunction with the pastor or director of Christian education. The church flow chart should be placed in a visible area of the school.

Pastor

↓

Pastoral Ministries (Deacons,Trustees, Deaconess, Music, etc.)

↓

Director of Christian Education

↓

Board of Christian Education

↓

Director of Ministries (Usually for paid positions-may not exist)

↓

Department Ministry Leaders

Ministries   Sunday Church School ↓

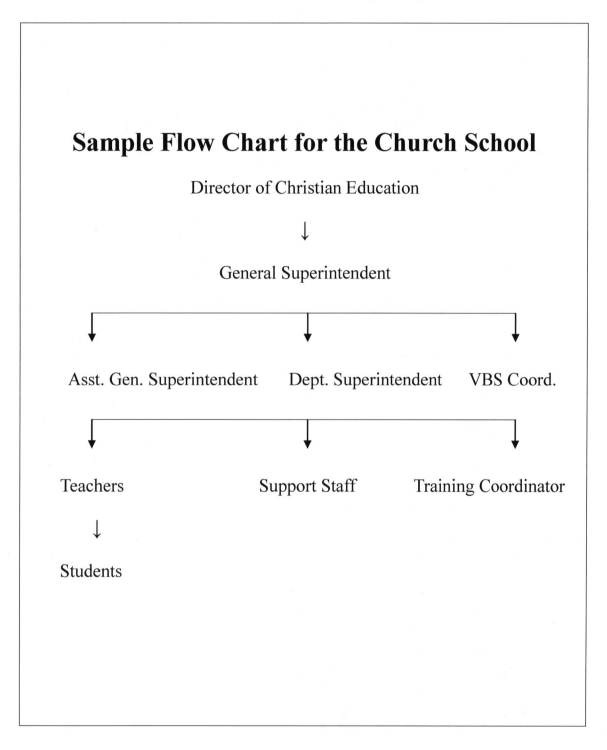

Sample Flow Chart for the Church School

Director of Christian Education

↓

General Superintendent

Asst. Gen. Superintendent   Dept. Superintendent   VBS Coord.

Teachers   Support Staff   Training Coordinator

↓

Students

FORM E: An Administrative Calendar Sample: Evaluation of Church School Needs

The church school will be evaluated each year. Prior to the end of the calendar year, the church school superintendent will report to the director of Christian education on: curriculum, student needs, and the number of teachers. The superintendent will report needs of the Sunday church school to the director of Christian education.

Recruiting Instructors and Prospective Teachers

Decide on a date to distribute instructor's and prospective teacher's applications and a deadline to receive them. Decide on a central location to receive applications. All instructors and prospective teachers should be required to complete an application. The superintendent should review and return this information to the director with suggestions.

Teacher In-Service Training

All teachers should be required to attend in-services training during the year. These in-services differ from prospective teacher training and should not substitute. In-services are scheduled times when teachers can update their skills. Speakers may be invited. Specific topics may be decided for the next three years.

Graduation Program for Prospective Teachers

The director should decide on the suggested program for graduation. The program should be given to both the superintendent and the director of Christian education for review. Upon recommendation, the director should then begin printing bulletins for the event.

- ❖ **Dates for Prospective Teachers Training**
- ❖ **Dates for Internship**
- ❖ **Dates for Recruiting Prospective Teachers**
- ❖ **Dates for Current Teacher Training**
- ❖ **Dates for Recruiting New Teachers**
- ❖ **Dates for Teacher Retreats**
- ❖ **Dates for Church School Picnic**
- ❖ **Dates for Leaders to Meet**
- ❖ **Dates for Teacher Meetings**
- ❖ **Dates for Church School Fun Nights**
- ❖ **Dates for Lesson Plans**
- ❖ **Dates for Opening and Closing of the School Year**
- ❖ **Dates for VBS**
- ❖ **Date for Promotional Exercises**
- ❖ **Dates for School Evangelism Project**
- ❖ **Dates for Open House**

FORM F: Job Descriptions

Job descriptions for superintendent, assistant superintendents, teachers, workers, and support staff (secretaries, etc.), applications for prospective teachers and new teachers, Evangelism Chair, instructors for prospective teachers, and VBS coordinator: may be developed by the superintendent in conjunction with the director of Christian education.
(See Dr. Sandidge's <u>STRATEGIES FOR THE DCE</u>.)

Form 1F

JOB TITLE: GENERAL SUPERINTENDENT OF THE CHURCH SCHOOL

JOB DESCRIPTION:
The General Superintendent will:

   ⇨ advise and monitor department superintendents
   ⇨ maintain school class teacher rosters and records of all church school activities
   ⇨ provide assessments and any final analysis of the school
   ⇨ seek ideas to enhance the school
   ⇨ plan proposed annual objectives and goals for the school and submit for DCE's consideration
   ⇨ propose an annual budget for the school and submit for DCE's consideration
   ⇨ meet with Assistant General Superintendents and Department Superintendent(s) to plan school administration and to discuss all school concerns, e.g., supplies, classroom and instruction concerns, teacher and student concerns
   ⇨ plan and submit to the DCE an annual calendar for consideration
   ⇨ attend board meetings
   ⇨ order materials in conjunction and approval from the DCE
   ⇨ report to the DCE education or pastor
   ⇨ monitor and distribute(or assign) curriculum materials
   ⇨ maintain school file key (One assistant superintendent and clerk may have a key)
   ⇨ supervise and be responsible for the entire church school
   ⇨ call meetings as needed

Form 2F

JOB TITLE: ASSISTANT SUPERINTENDENT(S)

JOB DESCRIPTION: Assistant Superintendent(s) will:

- ✓ adhere to the direction of the superintendent

- ✓ adhere to pastor and director of Christian education

- ✓ train teachers and perhaps prospective teachers (if no special administrator)

- ✓ review curriculum and make suggestions

- ✓ call grade level teacher meetings

- ✓ assist superintendent in needed duties: calendar planning, special projects, attendance, and school administration

Form 3F

JOB TITLE: CHURCH SCHOOL SUPPORT TEAM

JOB DESCRIPTION: Church School Support Team will:

♦ report to job assignment

♦ assist in making sure supplies are available

♦ assist teacher with meeting class needs

♦ report messages and deliveries

♦ work with students as needed, i.e. groups and creative projects

♦ collect and distribute class hand-outs

Form 3F-1

JOB TITLE: DEPARTMENT SECRETARIES

JOB DESCRIPTION: Department Secretaries will:

☐ report to the General Superintendent

☐ maintain attendance and offering records for the school department

☐ collect school offerings

☐ maintain department attendance and offering records

☐ submit attendance/offering envelopes to church clerk

Form 3F-2

JOB TITLE: **CLASS AND ASSISTANT SECRETARIES**

JOB DESCRIPTION: **Class and Assistant Secretaries will***:*

- record class attendance and collect class offering. Record attendance and offering sheet in provided envelopes.

- deliver attendance or offering envelopes to the department secretary.

- maintain and periodically update current class rosters.

- contact students who are regularly absent from class.

- report names of students who are sick and shut-in, hospitalizations or deaths in immediate families.

Form 3F-3

JOB TITLE: LIBRARIAN AND ASSISTANT LIBRARIAN

JOB DESCRIPTION: Librarian and Assistant Librarian will:

- periodically suggest supplementary instructional materials for classes

- organize school materials for each class

- arrange for distributing school material

Responsibilities

The School Statistician will:

- collect and update school class rosters from teachers

- collect weekly church attendance records from church clerk and prepare school attendance statistical spreadsheet reports at least quarterly

- collect enrollment forms for new school students report to General Superintendent and the DCE

Form 3F-4

JOB TITLE: VACATION BIBLE SCHOOL (VBS) COORDINATOR

JOB DESCRIPTION: The VBS Coordinator will:

- □ prepare a proposed plan of the VBS curriculum in conjunction with the General Superintendent of the school and submit to the DCE for approval

- □ suggest VBS material and promotional material to the General Superintendent and the DCE

- □ suggest VBS training for VBS teachers and staff to the General Superintendent and the DCE

- □ coordinate and supervise VBS classes and activities for all ages

- □ prepare a final summary for the General Superintendent and the DCE

- □ suggest to the Superintendent and the DCE a meal menu for VBS attendees

- □ make arrangements and get approval from the General Superintendent and DCE for all scheduled VBS field trips responsible to the General Superintendent and the DCE

- □ plan VBS fellowship

- □ determine music and worship and worship leaders

- □ suggest budget for crafts, recreations, and awards

Form 3F-5

JOB TITLE: **PROGRAM ADMINISTATOR FOR PROSPECTIVE AND CURRENT TEACHERTRAINING**

JOB DESCRIPTION: The Program Administrator will:

- in conjunction with the director of Christian education and church school superintendent, devise a separate calendar for prospective teacher training and current teacher training

- have the skills similar to an public school instructor

- possess administrative skills

- understand the church school teacher's instructional tasks

- recommend a three year syllabus and course offerings for prospective and current teachers

- leadership activities--participate in suggested activities when required

- create a calendar for all dates. Include dates for instructors, prospective teachers, dates for meeting with the superintendent and director of Christian education, and other announcements

- recruit instructors and require instructors to submit syllabi and outlines; recruit prospective teachers and recruit current teachers

- report to one of the following: General Superintendent, Director of Christian Education, or Director of Support Team. Varies from church to church.

Form 3F-6

**JOB TITLE: THE ELECTIVE COURSE OFFERING
                ADMINISTRATOR**

JOB DESCRIPTION: Elective Course—Offering

Administrator should:

- suggest elective course offerings and course descriptions for the next three years(decide how the elective courses will not interfere with regular classes—perhaps classes for one or two months that are held after church school to afford every person an opportunity to attend, teachers and students--This may mean to shorten regular class time and perhaps to delete the school overview to limit school time--one hour for electives and one hour for general instruction)
- recommends instructors and instructor's job descriptions for courses
- recommends dates for courses

FORM G: Sample Hours of Operation

The Landmark Church Sunday School will operate from 9 A.M. to 10:30 A.M. each Sunday morning, except for July. The Sunday school will not be opened during the last two weeks of July because of vacation.

FORM H: Sample Design of Classes/classrooms

Classes/classrooms are designed in the following manner:

Ages 1 to 3—Room 100

Ages 4 to 7—Room 101

Ages 8 to 12—Room 102

Ages 13 to 16—Room 103

Ages 17 to 20—Room 104

Ages 21 to 30—Room 105

Ages 31 to 40—Room 106

Ages 41 to 50—Room 107

Ages 51 to 60—Room 108

Ages 61 to 70—Room 109

Ages 71 and up—Room 110

Form I: Application for Prospective Teachers

Name: _____

Address: _____

City: _____ State:_____ Zip:_____

Telephone (home): _____Telephone (work): _____

Requirements:

One must be a Christian

⇨ One must attend a Bible class
⇨ One must obtain a Letter of Recommendation from a school teacher

Sunday school class you attend:_____

How long have you attended?_____

Teacher's name:_____

Envelope number:_____

Why are you interested in teaching?_____

Signature:_____

Date:_____

FORM J: Sample Agenda for Superintendents

♦ Devotion

♦ Report on teachers and classes

♦ Review calendar dates and events

♦ Review and discuss goals and objectives for church school

♦ Discuss upcoming teacher training

♦ Discuss progress of teachers and students

♦ Review roster of new teachers and students

♦ Review new church members and present members not attending classes

♦ Review entire church school needs

♦ Closing remarks and prayer

FORM K: Sample Discipline Policies for Administrators, Teachers, and Students

All disciplinary action will be at the discretion of the pastor or director of Christian education. Each case may differ.

- Teacher misconduct

- Student misconduct

- Insubordination

- Violation of school requirements

- Other reasons

    a) Poor attendance
    b) Lack of preparation
    c) Attitude
    d) Not promoting "good" learning

FORM L: Request Information: Names, Addresses, and Contacts for Church School Record

Have a list such as:

➢ **Names, phone numbers, and addresses of the following church leaders:**

  ➢ pastor

  ➢ director of Christian education

  ➢ ministerial staff

  ➢ deacons

  ➢ deaconesses

  ➢ trustees

  ➢ directors

  ➢ all ministry leaders

Also maintain a list of names, phone numbers, and addresses for school superintendents, teachers, substitutes, and support staff.

(See the book **Strategies For the Director of Christian Education**.)

FORM M: Learn Financial Procedures

a. Know all financial guidelines for the school

b. Know the guidelines for signing requisitions (requests)

c. Know steps for requesting funds

d. Know deadlines

e. Copies of every submission should be kept by the superintendent

f. Some churches request that the DCE is the last one to sign and approve ministry requisitions. Clearly comprehend your responsibilities and limitations

FORM N: Sample Dress Code for the Church School

We leaders, support staff, and teachers will abide by the following dress code:

1. No jeans or clothing that is too short-above finger tip of hands, with arm hanging by your side

2. No clothing that distracts the Gospel from being presented or received

3. No tight clothing that distracts teaching or learning

4. No tennis shoes, if other shoes are available

5. No halter tops

6. No head bands

7. No clothing with words that display a non-Christian message

FORM O: Curriculum Review and Curriculum Materials

Who develops the curriculum for the church? The DCE provides advice but the DCE should not develop the total curriculum. **The DCE should guide the Board of Christian Education of the select committee to develop the curriculum for the Department of Christian Education.** The superintendent should share in developing curriculum for the church school. The superintendent may:

1. establish a date for the review

2. elect a committee: teachers, students, ministerial staff person, and perhaps a director of Christian education. A seven or a twelve member committee may work

3. inform committee of duties and give at least a two weeks notice for the review

4. decide on the location, tables, and evaluation form

5. order materials from at least three publishers. Also use current literature

6. decide on a time to have discussions and to draw conclusions

7. make recommendation to pastor and director of Christian education

Note: There is no standing committee. Select a new committee for each review

FORM P: Bible Version(s)

The superintendent may keep the following in mind:

1. Decide on a Bible version that is appropriate for the age, class, or understanding level.

2. Provide a trial test for one month. Allow students to study from two recommended versions before adopting or having students to purchase a version. The superintendent needs to consider copying pages for students to use during the trial month.

3. Allow students to vote on a version.

4. Provide recommendations to pastor and director of Christian education.

5. Maintain extra copies.

FORM Q: Purchasing Material(s)

All material will be purchased by the superintendent. Complete this form to suggest materials.

Name of teacher_____

Materials requested_____

List quantities for materials_____

Purpose for request _____

Date of request _____

Where can one purchase materials? Be specific.

FORM R: Using Supplementary Materials

I _____ (teacher) agree to only use supplementary material that promotes my teaching points, all which adhere to the church's Mission Statement, pastor's vision, and church school's Mission Statement. The superintendent will be consulted if in question: Using inappropriate literature is a reason for action.

Signature of teacher _____

Date of agreement _____

FORM S: Sample Opening School Day Agenda

- Devotions

- Introductions: Superintendent

    - Assistant Superintendent(s)

    - Support Staff

- Overview of Theme:

- Activity:

- What Lies Ahead:

- Final Directions:

- Review of Handbook—Rules

- Pastoral comments

- Closing

FORM T: Sample End of the School Year Closing Day Agenda (only for support staff)

- Devotions:

- Promotional exercise directions:

- Final student assessments:

- The beginning of the next school year order

- Teachers' and support team recognitions

- Final words

FORM U: Sample Promotional Exercises

- Processional

- Devotional Period

- Opening Statement

- Opening Choir Selection

- Scripture

- Prayer

- Choir Selection

- Guest Speaker

- Promotions Conferred /Certificates

- Presented

- Special Recognitions

- Pastoral Comments

- Recessional

- Benediction

FORM V: Confidential Records and Folders

I _____ agree that all student records and folders are considered confidential. All phone calls must be documented in folders. All folders are kept by each teacher. Violation of student records or folders may result in dismissal.

_____ Signature

_____ Date

Note: Each teacher signs this form

FORM W: Sample Missed Classes or Assignments

All missed class assignments must be made up within one month. A student missing twelve class assignments, (unless assignments are made up), will not be allowed to participate in promotional exercises.

Form X: Sample Attendance and Substitute Policies

<u>Attendance</u>

1. Teachers should check student attendance daily

2. Teachers should contact home if students are absent for one month

3. Teacher should keep attendance records

<u>Substitutes</u>

1. Teachers should follow the church school instructions for contacting substitutes

FORM Y: Sample Evangelism Guidelines

Evangelism Guidelines

- **The Announcement**
  John 1:35-40
  John 1:41-42
  John 1:43-51
- **The Condition**
  John 8:31
  John 13:35
  John 15:8
- **Find Those Who Will Listen**
  Matthew 10:5-6
- **Do Not Impose**
  Matthew 10:34-38
- **Remain a Team**
  Mark 6:7
- **Speak with Authority and Power**
  Mark 6:7
  Matthew 10:1
  Luke 9:1
- **Remember Who You Represent**
  John 13:20
  Matthew 13:20
- **Remember Scriptures**
  Romans 3:23
  Romans 6:23
  Roman 5:8
  Romans 10:9

Steps for Evangelizing
- Discover Self
- Decide on Perimeter for Witnessing
- Seek Information About the Community
- Flyers
- Home Bible Study
- Media
- Door to Door
- Telephone

Y cont'd

The Steps to Commitment

- Admitting one is a sinner

- Ask what hinders being saved

- **Plan of Salvation**

  a) Belief in God: Romans 10:4;

  b) Confession: Matthew 10:32, Romans 10:9-10;

  c) Repent: Luke 13:5;

  d) Prayer of Confession

  e) Receive: John 1:2; Romans 10:13;

  f) Obedience: John 14:15

FORM Z: Sample Mentoring Guidelines

Twelve Suggested Guidelines

- ✓ Be a wise advisor
- ✓ Be trustworthy
- ✓ Both the mentor and mentee should benefit from the experience
- ✓ Mentors only guide individuals
- ✓ Mentors are not professional counselors, social workers, playmates, or friends.
- ✓ Do not break promises
- ✓ Be consistent
- ✓ Do not bestow gifts or money
- ✓ Maintain confidentiality
- ✓ Be on time
- ✓ Be a good listener
- ✓ Do not invite mentee to your home

FORM AA: Sample Retreats

A retreat is to relax, rejuvenate, and to be free from workshops or stressful activities. The agenda must incorporate "fun" things.

FORM BB: Field Trip Permissions

I _____ give permission for my son/daughter to travel to _____ with the New Run Baptist Church School. The church school will not be responsible for any committed acts that shall cause liability due to student involvement.

Other Information

Departing from _____

Departure time _____

Returning time _____

Clothing desired _____

Suggested funds _____

The cost per student will be _____

Price includes: _____

Signature of parent _____

Signature of student _____

Date_____

FORM CC: Emergencies

Sample Medical and Liability Release

(Should be printed on the church's letterhead)

It is also recommended to seek medical forms from physicians in your state. Medical laws may change from state to state.

Name of Student_____ Age _____
Address _____
City/State _____Zip _____Phone _____
In emergency, notify _____
Phone _____
Health history:
*Allergies: List any
*Other conditions: __Heart _____Frequent colds
*Chronic conditions:____Asthma __Frequent Diabetes __Epilepsy
*Physical problems:____High Blood Pressure
*Other
If you checked any of the above, please give details (i.e., include normal treatment of allergic reactions):
*Date of last tetanus shot:
Name and dosage of any medications that must be taken:
*Any swimming restrictions:_____Yes___No
*Any activity restrictions:____Yes____No
*What restrictions?
*Anything else that we should know?
Name and address of your primary care doctor?
Address of your doctor:
Telephone number of your doctor:
Permission to take student to ER ____Yes ____No

Signature _____
Date _____

FORM DD: Sample Lesson Overview

Components for the Lesson Plan

Every lesson plan has a beginning, middle, and an end.

1) Goal

2) Main Idea

3) Objective

4) The Lesson Design

Step One: Beginning

Step Two: Stating Objective

Step Three: Introducing the Content

Step Four: Modeling the Content

Step Five: Discovering the Content

Step Six: Relating to the Content

Step Seven: Concluding the Content

Step Eight: Reinforcing the Content

Teachers who cannot write: Meet with the superintendent at a designated time to orally give an overview.

Teachers who have limited skills: Write title of lesson, scriptural references, summary of what will be taught, and discuss activity to be used.

FORM EE: Sample Evaluations for Church School Leaders

Evaluation for Superintendent and Assistant(s) Superintendents

Evaluation Form for the Superintendent and Assistant Superintendent

1. Is the leader on time for meetings? Yes or No
2. Is the leader doing a good job? Yes or No
3. Does the leader maintain peaceful relationships with participants? Yes or No
4. Is there good communication between the superintendents and participants? Yes or No
5. Does the leader accept authoritative assignments? Yes or No
6. Comment on two positive observations of the superintendent.
   a)
   b)
7. Comment on two observations of the superintendent that need improvement
   a)
   b)

Signature of observer: _____

Name of the person observed: _____

Name of ministry: _____

Date observed: _____

Note: The director of Christian education or pastor observes the superintendent.

FORM FF: Sample Open House Day Agenda

❖ Devotions

❖ Each teacher and worker should go to designated booth

❖ Attendance sign in

❖ Booth set up

FORM GG: Sample Special Mission's Project Day

- ➢ Devotions

- ➢ Directions for Missions Day

- ➢ Travel

- ➢ Departure and return time

- ➢ Special instructions

- ➢ Review of "How to proceed"

- ➢ Prayer

FORM HH: Church Statistician

Application for Prospective Teachers

Name: _____

Address: _____

City: _____ State: _____ Zip: _____

Telephone (home): _____ Telephone (work): _____

Requirements:

1. One must be a Christian

2. One must attend a Bible class

3. One must obtain a Letter of Recommendation from a teacher

Sunday school class you attend: _____

How long have you attended this church:?_____

Teacher's name: _____

Envelope number: _____

Why are you interested in teaching? _____

List any experience with desired age group. _____

_____

Signature: _____

Date: _____

FORM II: Sample Meeting Agenda for Superintendents and Church School

- **Monthly or Bi-monthly Meetings are:**

Date: <u>1st Saturday</u> at 10 A.M. Meeting with teachers, support staff, and church school leaders

Date: <u>3rd Saturday</u> at 10 A.M. Meeting with church school leaders

- **The First School Meeting with Department Superintendents**

  1. Devotions

  2. Review current school status: calendar, classes, pastoral concerns

  3. Review student attendance

  4. Review classroom learning

  5. Review teaching staff

  6. Review each superintendent report

Minutes of each meeting should be given to superintendent no later than the following week.

Note: Elect a secretary for this group. Use above agenda for Assistant Superintendents. Review all assignments.

FORM JJ: Sample Meeting Agenda for Director of Christian Education with the Superintendent

The First School Meeting: Superintendent and Pastor or Director of Christian Education

Note: A secretary should be elected to take minutes at all meetings. Typed minutes should be provided to the director of Christian education or pastor. The pastor or the director of Christian education leads this meeting.

1. Devotions and introductions
2. Purpose of meeting—To begin planning for the year
3. A get-to-know-you game or ice-breaker
4. Distribute a copy of the upcoming annual Christian education calendar and budget
5. Discuss Mission Statement of the church, pastor's Vision Statement, goals and objectives for the church school
6. Discuss ways to survey the church school, teachers, support staff, students, and church members to learn needs and desired learning in the church school
7. Begin planning—Plan for developing or revising handbook—Discuss deadlines
8. Review or establish at least two ministry meeting dates for all ministry leaders to meet with the superintendent to discuss common church needs
9. Prayer
10. Discuss expectations of superintendent, assistant superintendent(s), teachers, support staff, and students
11. Ask superintendent to share some fun things they liked last year
12. Remind superintendent of teamwork
13. Preachers and speakers for the entire year must be approved by the DCE or pastor
14. Field trips and workshops—All field trips and workshops should have: a purpose, learning experience, and relate to ministry—Field trips and workshops must be approved by superintendent and the DCE/or the pastor
15. Discuss what should take place at each class session
16. Discuss monthly reports to DCE (Pastor collects report if no DCE.)
17. Announce next meeting date
18. Benediction

FORM KK: **Sample Meeting Agenda for Superintendent Meeting with Teachers and Support Team**

1. Devotions
2. Ice breaker
3. Review previous meeting minutes
4. Distribute a questionnaire to learn about needs and desires (Return results at next meeting.)
5. Elect compilers to work on sections of the handbook and present the steps. Remind compilers to submit draft by a deadline. Discuss how superintendent will review and make suggestions for improving sections, elect blind readers, and decide on due dates
6. Select prayer partners—select two or three to be prayer partners for the year. Discuss responsibilities
7. Superintendent discusses job descriptions, length of service, service agreement, and lesson plan format
8. The church school group prays
9. Announce next meeting
10. Benediction

FORM LL: **Other Suggested Meetings Sample Agenda with Teachers and Support Team**

1. Teachers' and Support Team Second Meeting
   a. The current teacher training handbook first review
   b. The current church school needs
   c. Current classes and teachers serving
   d. Current student enrollment
   e. The church school calendar

2. Teachers' and Support Team Third Meeting
   a. Second review of handbook
   b. Classroom concerns
   c. Other duties

3. Teacher Training Administrator(s) Report

4. Director of Christian Education and Pastoral Comments

Forms to Use in My Handbook

Forms to Use in My Handbook

Forms to Use in My Handbook

Forms to Use in My Handbook

Forms to Use in My Handbook

CHAPTER THREE:
A CURRENT TEACHER'S
HANDBOOK

CHAPTER THREE:
A CURRENT TEACHER'S HANDBOOK

A current teacher's handbook is for current teachers. This handbook gives the current teacher an overview of teaching.

A teacher's handbook will diminish many questions that teachers propose. Teachers may use this handbook as a guide, a reminder, and as an overview of the teaching assignment.

A Mini Handbook for Current Teachers Might Include:

⇨ Application for Teachers

⇨ Job Description Agreement

⇨ Length of Service Agreement

⇨ A Remembrance of Words for "TEACHER"

⇨ Sample Get-to-Know You Form

⇨ Teacher Training Workshops (In-Services)

⇨ Retreats

⇨ Teacher's Self-Evaluation

⇨ Evaluation for Current Teachers

Keep in mind goals and objectives when preparing this handbook. *The goal or purpose might be* to assist Christian teachers and leaders in the church school classroom. *The overall objective might be*: Teachers and leaders will be able to identify the structure and operation of the church school.

Application for Teachers

Name:_____

Address:_____

City:_____ State:_____ Zip:_____

Telephone (home):_____ Telephone (work):_____

Requirements:

- ☐ One must be a Christian.
- ☐ One must attend a Bible class.
- ☐ One must obtain a Letter of Recommendation from your teacher.

Sunday school class you attend: _____

How long have you attended: _____

Envelope number: _____

Why are you interested in teaching:? _____

Have you completed the prospective teacher's training course:?_____

What teacher supervised you?:_____

Have you read and agree to the teacher's job description:?_____

What age/grade do you desire to teach:?_____

When will you be available to begin an assignment:?_____

Signature: _____

Date: _____

JOB TITLE: CHURCH SCHOOL TEACHERS

RESPONSIBILITIES OF CHURCH SCHOOL TEACHERS

JOB DESCRIPTION: Teachers will teach the Word of God

<u>The Teacher will:</u>

1) be a born again Christian who believes the Holy Bible to be the inspired Word of God and support the doctrinal statement of this church
2) spend time in prayer, devotions, and pray for students
3) attend Bible study
4) have a burning desire to teach and be teachable
5) be responsible for a decorative room
6) maintain attendance records and inquire about those who frequently miss class
7) attend teacher's meetings
8) attend in-service training or workshops
9) up-date certification by enrolling in new phases of prospective teacher training
10) be willing to modify teaching methods and learn new ideas
11) use the materials set forth by the church school, including Bible version, and school text
12) separate personal opinions from teaching content
13) prepare lesson plans as recommended
14) be on time for classes
15) read and study God's Word
16) report to the Superintendent
17) adhere to the Holy Spirit and be a good listener and doer
18) love the age group
19) be committed to a flexible schedule
20) be receptive to constructive criticisms and maintain a positive attitude
21) be humble, meek, caring, and model a Christian life
22) be willing to follow the mission statement, goals, and objectives of the church and church school
23) believe in pastor's vision and teaching and follow pastor's leadership

24) have leadership ability
25) have good rapport with students and co-workers
26) be a team player
27) contribute to the church: tithing and love offerings
28) help students discover their purpose and prepare students to teach others how to discover purpose
29) have the right character I Timothy 3:2-7 & Titus 1:7-9

I have read, understand, and will adhere to the responsibilities of church school teachers.

_____Name of teacher

_____ Date signed

A Remembrance of Words for Teacher

➤ Didaskolos   I Timothy 2:7 Often used by Jesus

➤ Didasko   Acts 2:42; 2 Timothy 3:16 "Doctrine"

➤ Paideuo   Ephesians 6:4 "Guidance and Training" and Parental Teaching
2 Timothy 3:16 Value of Inspired Word

➤ Katecheo   Only used by Luke: Luke 1:4 Acts 18:25: 21:21 and Paul Romans 2:18; 1 Corinthians 14:19; Galatians 6:6 We got the word catechism and catechumen (learner) from it

➤ Noutheteo   1 Corinthians 4:14; 1 Corinthians 10:11; Ephesians 6:4 and Colossians 3:16 "Shape the mind" which is translated "admonish"

➤ Maltheteuo   To disciple. Only in the Gospels and Acts of Apostles

➤ Oikodomeo   "Edify or build up" 1 Corinthians 3:9; 1 Corinthians 8:1; 1 Thessalonians 5:1; 1 Peter 2:5

➤ Paratithemi   "Set before or place beside" 1Timothy 1:18; 2 Timothy 2:2   "Commit"

➢ Ektithemi   Acts 11:4; Acts 18:26; Acts 28:23; Explain facts in "logical order" or to "expound"

➢ Hodegeo   Acts 1: 16 "Guiding"; John 16: 13; Acts 8:31; Revelation 7:17

Sample Get-to-Know You Form for Teachers and Workers

♦ Your name_____
♦ Your address_____
♦ Your home phone_____
♦ Your home fax_____
♦ Your work phone_____
♦ Your cell phone_____
♦ Your E-mail address_____
♦ Name of ministry_____
♦ Tell me about your experience and/or desired experience for the ministry.
♦ Discuss your past experiences associated with this ministry.
♦ What are your special skills, gifts and talents?
♦ What in particular do you desire to do in this ministry?

Teacher Training Workshops
Conducted by Teacher Training Coordinator

Workshops are always needed for teachers. Questions about workshops: What is a workshop for teachers? Should all teachers be required to attend workshops? How frequently asked should workshops be held?

What Is a Workshop for Teachers?

A workshop for teachers is no more than in-service training. It is a time to provide service to teachers. Teachers are enlightened about Christian living by attending motivational workshops, which provide tools for Christian teaching; workshops help teachers identify student needs. It does not matter how long one has been teaching, in-services should provide a new perspective for teachers. Workshops should help rehabilitate, stimulate, and motivate the teacher.

Should All Teachers Be Required to Attend Workshops?

It is very important for all teachers to attend workshops. Keep in mind that volunteer teachers need free time. Too many workshops can deplete one's ability to freely provide services. Leaders must understand that teaching is not the only responsibility of the teacher.

Workshop Agendas

The agenda should always include devotions, a focus or spiritual renewal, and some particular content. Brief agendas usually serve best.

Who Plans for the Workshops?

The director of Christian education and the superintendent should plan for workshops. In many cases, the superintendent submits a proposal to the director of Christian education. Some directors of Christian education prefer a joint planning session. Superintendents may or may not involve assistant superintendents. The director informs the pastor. Suggestions from teachers should always be invited.

Retreats

A retreat is a time to relax and refresh. It is a time for teachers to explore their own spiritual dimension. It is also a time to reflect about "Who am I?" and "Whose am I?" We reflect what we believe. Many times one's belief will be rekindled when one leaves the present work environment. **Retreats should be held away from the work site.**

Retreats are needed because the teacher will not excel in teaching if overstressed or overworked. It is wise to have at least two retreats per year, perhaps about three months after the new school year and three months before the end of the school year.

In helping others, teachers need to show students that God also helps the teacher. As Evangelist Shirley Caesar once stated, "When we bring forth the spirituality of teaching and learning, we help students honor life's most meaningful questions."

God might not grant what we want or claim because what we want or claim might not be what we need. He provides desires, but we should not demand desires "right now." It might be tomorrow! Teachers need to understand that students too have many desires.

Seven Suggested Retreats for Teachers

➢ Take a trip to spiritual center—You can use the Internet and/or travel agency to find one

➢ Rent a room in a nice hotel and have guest motivators lead sessions

➢ Go to the beach for relaxation near water

➢ Visit a mountain area for serenity

➢ Go on a local cruise with private space, speakers, and dinners

➢ Plan a two-night event, including a time for massage therapy, games, and a "get-to-know-you-better" time

➢ Provide multicultural workshops--incorporate other cultures

A TEACHER'S SELF-EVALUATION GUIDE

1. Assess yourself in each of the following:
    A. I understand the stated goals of the religious education program as a whole
    _____Always _____Nearly Always _____I need to work on this
    B. The content of my teaching is in accord with theses goals
    _____Always _____Nearly Always _____I need to work on this
    C. The methods of my teaching are in accord with these goals.
    _____Always _____Nearly Always _____I need to work on this

2. Organization
    `A. I plan sessions in advance, familiarizing myself with each lesson's content, method; and, adapting it as needed for my students.
    _____Always _____Nearly Always _____I need to work on this
    B. I request, collect, and test all needed supplies and resources well in advance.
    _____Always _____Nearly Always _____I need to work on this
    C. I proceed in class in an orderly fashion.
    _____Always _____Nearly Always _____I need to work on this

3. Attendance and Punctuality
    A. I myself have close to 100 percent attendance and I make arrangement when I need to have a substitute.
    _____Always _____Nearly Always _____I need to work on this
    B. I am punctual, arriving in class in advance of the first student.
    _____Always _____Nearly Always _____I need to work on this

4. Teacher-Student relations
    A. I am in touch with the contemporary situation and the circumstances of my students.
    _____Always _____Nearly Always _____I need to work on this
    B. I try to understand my students' needs and actions.
    _____Always _____Nearly Always _____I need to work on this
    C. In class, I cultivate a pleasant disposition, maintaining enthusiasm, calmness, and firmness.
    _____Always _____Nearly Always _____I need to work on this
    D. I am able to manage the class as a whole.
    _____Always _____Nearly Always _____I need to work on this

5. Creativity and Growth
    A. I actively seek and consider suggestions from others regarding my teaching.
    _____Always _____Nearly Always _____I need to work on this
    B. I am increasing in the creative use of teaching materials.
    _____Always _____Nearly Always _____I need to work on this
    C. I read one or more books annually to enrich my teaching.
    _____Always _____Nearly Always _____I need to work on this
    D. I attend one or more teacher's workshop annually.
    _____Always _____Nearly Always _____I need to work on this

6. Cooperation and Collaboration
    A. I attend regular teachers' meetings.
    _____Always _____Nearly Always _____I need to work on this
    B. I collaborate when needed to develop goals, choose curriculum, evaluate programs, etc.
    _____Always _____Nearly Always _____I need to work on this
    C. I work closely and cooperatively with other staff members.
    _____Always _____Nearly Always _____I need to work on this
    D. I maintain open communications with the parents of my students.
    _____Always _____Nearly Always _____I need to work on this
TAKEN FROM: HARPER'S ENCYCLOPEDIA OF RELIGIOUS EDUCATION

Evaluation for Current Teachers

Date:_____ Grade____

Name of Teacher:_____

Name of Observer:_____

Time:_____

Classroom Observations: Each teacher will be rated on a scale from one to twenty-one. Twenty-one is the highest, demonstrating excellence. Place and "X" for "not observed."

_____ 1. Classroom arrangement
_____ 2. Creativity in the classroom
_____ 3. Students' response to teaching
_____ 4. All students were involved in the learning process
_____ 5. The Bible of God's Word was the major source for teaching
_____ 6. The teacher displayed a warm attitude
_____ 7. Students were well disciplined
_____ 8. Students appeared to have a high comprehension level
_____ 9. Students were excited to learn
_____10. Teacher had good lesson plans
_____11. Teacher stated the objectives clearly
_____12. Teacher reviewed the former lesson
_____13. No student was tardy
_____14. Teaching method was understood
_____15. Lesson was related to real life
_____16. Teacher started and ended the class on time
_____17. Teacher allowed for learning styles of students
_____18. Teacher allowed for individual instruction
_____19. Teacher's outward appearance of spirituality was high
_____20. Teacher was a good motivator
_____21. There was a blackboard and chalk for the teacher

Scoring: Add the total number of X's
20-21—Excellent
18-19—Good
16-17—Fair
10-15—Close monitoring needed; classes and workshops recommended

Plans for Current Teachers

Plans for Current Teachers

Plans for Current Teachers

Plans for Current Teachers

Plans for Current Teachers

CHAPTER FOUR:
A PROSPECTIVE TEACHER'S
HANDBOOK

CHAPTER FOUR:
A PROSPECTIVE TEACHER'S HANDBOOK

This handbook will assist prospective teachers in understanding prospective teacher training. It will provide an overview for training prospective teachers. Prospective teachers will clearly understand their roles.

A Mini Handbook for Prospective Teachers Might Include:

➢ **Application for Prospective Teacher Training Instructors**

➢ **Application for Prospective Teachers**

➢ **Job Description**

➢ **The Calendar**

➢ **The Training Syllabus**

➢ **The Internship**

➢ **The Evaluation**

➢ **Graduation Requirements**

JOB TITLE: INSTRUCTOR OF PROSPECTIVE TEACHER TRAINING

JOB DESCRIPTION: **The instructor who leads training for prospective teachers**

The instructor of prospective teacher training should be:

- a Christian
- in good church standing
- a tither or plan to become a tither
- a Bible study student/teacher for the past year
- a Sunday school student/teacher for the past year
- a previous teacher/teaching experience
- willing to teach in a Christian setting
- able to take advice from others
- able to submit requested materials in a timely fashion
- one who keeps appointments
- able to report assignments on time

Application for Teacher Training Instructors

Please check all subjects in which you have an interest in teaching.

Session One: The Church School

___1. Mission of the Church and Church School

___2. Beliefs of the Church and the Denomination

___3. Objectives for the Church School

___4. History of Christian Education

Session Two: The Teacher

___1. Roles of the Teacher

___2. Self-Discipline

___3. Laws of the Teacher

Session Three: The Student

___1. Human Growth and Development

___2. Spiritual Growth and Development

___3. Life Issues in the African American Community

___4. Discipline and the Student

___5. Review Spiritual Gifts

___6. Review Purpose in Teachers and Students and How to "Discover Purpose"

Session Four: The Curriculum

___1. Activities Related to the Lesson

___2. Real Life Subjects

___3. Biblical Principles

___4. Biblical Subjects

Session Five: The Teaching

___1. Teaching in the Setting

___2. Individual Needs

___3. Planning the Lesson

___4. Lesson Components and Lesson Design

___5. The Handicap and Disabled Student (learning disabilities)

Session Six: The Discussion about Age Groups

___1. Children

___2. Youth

___3. Young Adults

___4. Adults

___5. Seniors

Application for Prospective Teachers

Name: _____

Address: _____

City:_____ State:_____ Zip:_____

Telephone (home):_____ Telephone (work):_____

Requirements:

1. One must be a Christian
2. One must attend Bible study
3. One must obtain a Letter of Recommendation from the practicum teacher
4. One must have good church attendance
5. One must possess teaching skills
6. One must like students

Sunday school class attended: _____

How long since you attended? _____

Teacher's name: _____

Envelope number: _____

Why are you interested in teaching? _____

Signature: _____

Date:_____

JOB TITLE: PROSPECTIVE TEACHER TRAINING

Job Description: To seek a possible teaching position

The Prospective Teacher:

- is a Christian
- attends church school or Bible class for at least one year
- is in good church standing
- is willing to teach the intended age group
- is a tither
- is willing to adhere to the doctrine of the church and denomination
- is a good planner
- keeps appointments and is on time
- has a humble Spirit
- takes advice from others
- does what ever is needed to complete the teaching task
- has good disciplinary skills; and
- is able to work with other teachers

Prospective Teacher Training Calendar

Objective: Prospective teachers will learn the recruiting methods for prospective teachers by reviewing the church school calendar.

Six months prior to training-recruitment of prospective teachers, consider:

* Pulpit announcements
* Bulletin and bulletin board announcements
* Personal contact with those who might meet requirements
* Newsletter announcements
* Praying for the right prospective teacher

Four months prior to training:

* Prospective teacher selection-This selection may be done by pastor, director of Christian education, superintendent, or any combination of selected persons

Three months prior to training:

* Prospective teachers declare grade-level interests
* Teacher training program handbook given to selected prospective teachers
* Prospective teachers register to visit Sunday church school classes

Decide on dates for the following:

Prospective teacher training—training with fewer sessions help prospective teachers recall facts and learn them in a consistent, systematic order. Prospective teacher training may be completed in five sessions. Prospective teachers could meet every other week for four to five hours and have thirty minutes for lunch.

Two months prior to training:

* Remind prospective teachers to review the syllabus, the handbook, and read suggested books.

One month prior to training:

* Send a reminder for training at least one month prior to prospective teachers beginning training date.

* Decide on dates for the following:

Teacher internship date (Three months are suggested for the internship.)

A Suggested Teacher Training Syllabus for Prospective Teachers

Leaders for this training should require all students to read books that will help them understand the content and the role of teaching. Short summaries of content learned should be turned in at the first class session. The following heading may be taught during prospective teacher training; one heading per session.

Topics for Prospective Teacher's Workshops

- **The Church and Sunday Church School**

The Syllabus Review:

1. Pastor's Goals and Mission of the Church and Sunday Church School
2. Baptist Beliefs
3. Goals and Objective for the Sunday Church School
4. History of Christian Education
5. New Testament Educational Terms

- **The Teacher**

6. Laws of Teaching
7. Roles of the Teacher
8. Self-discipline for Teachers
9. Teacher Commitment
10. Christian Teaching
11. Bible Teaching
12. Prayer
13. Curriculum
14. General Supplies
15. Supplementary Supplies

- **The Student**

16. Review of Human Growth Development
17. Review of Spiritual Growth Development
18. Life Issues in the African American Community
19. Discipline and the Student

- **The Teaching**

20. Teaching Methods
21. Biblical Principles

22. Individual Needs
23. Planning the Lesson
24. Lesson Components and Lesson Design
25. The Handicapped and Disabled Students

• **Various Age Groups and the Practicum**

26. Children
27. Youth
28. Young Adults
29. Adults
30. Senior Citizens
31. Internship

Internships for Prospective Teachers

An internship is a time for prospective teachers to get firsthand classroom teaching experience under the direction of a current teacher. The internship should last for three months to give the prospective teacher a variety of experiences. The classroom teacher and the program director closely monitor the prospective teacher. The duties of the prospective teacher should not replace the duties of the classroom teacher. The classroom teacher should remain in the classroom, perhaps, working on additional classroom projects.

• The internship (discuss dates)
• Each student will teach at least three lessons during the three-month internship
• All three-lesson plans should be turned in and approved by the supervising teacher at least four weeks before each class is taught. The supervising teacher will return all plans and corrections two weeks before class is taught

Evaluation of Prospective Teachers

Evaluation of the prospective teacher is very important for training. The evaluation should be written by the supervising teacher, program training director, and perhaps the director of Christian education. A superintendent should be fair and inform the prospective teacher, in a Christian way that he or she is or is not ready for teaching. A certificate should not be given to those who do not successfully complete the training. Usually a person knows if he or she is not ready for the task. Many members are only experimenting with this venture and may not have a call for the task.

The Evaluation

- All prospective teachers should be scheduled for teaching evaluation reviews within two to three weeks of final completion of training
- The director of Christian education and the General Superintendent or Departmental Superintendents, or any combination thereof, and the classroom teacher may evaluate the student prospective teacher
- A copy of all prospective teacher evaluations will be given to the General Superintendent and final copies given to the director of Christian education within one week following evaluations
- Completing the program does not promise a teaching position in a church school—Positions are determined by the needs of the church school—Names of those who successfully complete the training and are not given a position may be placed on a waiting list to be considered as future teachers or substitute teachers
- Completion of the training program will provide teachers with "requirements met" for teaching in your church school

Graduation Requirements

Prospective teachers must satisfactorily complete all reading assignments, internships, and attend all training classes to meet graduation requirements.

Prospective Teacher Internship Evaluation Sheet

Date:_____ Class:_____ Evaluator's Name:_____
Prospective Teacher's Name:_____
Assigned Class Teacher's Name:_____

Part I: Teaching Skills

Teacher Preparedness:

1. Arrived on time _____yes _____no
2. Was prepared to teach the lesson _____yes _____no

Lesson Aim:

3. Stated the lesson aim(s) clearly _____yes _____no
4. Stated the lesson objectives(s) clearly _____yes _____no

Introducing the Lesson:

5. Introduced the lesson creatively _____yes _____no
6. The students appeared to be interested in the lesson introduction _____yes _____no

Lesson Context and Background:

7. Presented adequate background to the lesson Scriptures, such as the author of the Scripture, when it was written and why, to whom the Scripture was written, and what occurred in earlier Scripture passages _____yes _____no
8. Provided background information relevant to the lesson, such as daily and life customs and practices of the time period, meanings of objects, symbols, holidays and festivals, kinship relationships, etc _____yes _____no

Lesson Content:

9. Explained clearly the meaning of the lesson Scriptures _____yes _____no

10. Able to group lesson Scriptures and present scriptural themes and instructional intent _____yes _____no

Lesson Application:

11. Connected scriptural meaning to the lives of the students and discussed how Scriptures apply to students' lives _____yes _____no

Follow Up Assignment:

12. Students were given an assignment to apply the lesson to their lives _____yes _____no

Part II: Communications Skills

Interaction with Students:

13. Teacher was open-minded and friendly with students _____yes_____no
14. Encouraged students to participate in the lesson by asking questions and allowing students to voice their own opinions _____yes _____no
15. Accepted and corrected students' responses in positive ways _____yes _____no

Use of Audiovisuals:

16. Used visuals such as charts, written material, maps, objects, etc _____yes _____no
17. (Optional) Used auditory media such as compact discs, videos, audiocassettes, etc _____yes _____no

15-17—Excellent
12-14—Good
9-11—Fair
0-9—Needs Improvement

Total score for this prospective teacher:_____
Comments:

Plans for Prospective Teachers

Plans for Prospective Teachers

Plans for Prospective Teachers

Plans for Prospective Teachers

Plans for Prospective Teachers

CHAPTER FIVE:
THE SUPPORT TEAM

CHAPTER FIVE:

THE SUPPORT TEAM

A church school needs different types of workers to maintain an effective Sunday school or church school. Everybody plays a significant role in shaping learning. The teacher assistant, the custodial staff, the librarian, the teacher, church school leaders, secretaries, statistician, media, and other staff are a team. Even though school church leaders and teachers are not considered under the leadership of the Support Team, surely everyone makes up the entire team.

A support team is one that assists with functions other than serving as lead teacher or directly as church school leader. Not all support team members teach. There are varied assignments, other than teaching, which require the support team. **This ministry comes under the department of Christian education. This ministry provides support to all ministries, including the church school.** If no such ministry exists under the department of Christian education, surely the superintendent needs this ministry.

The support team ministry leader directs the entire team. The department of Christian education provides general training for this ministry. The church school, per the assignment, may recommend specific training for the church school. Training will vary from church to church. The important thing is to provide clear "instructions" for the support team. This team may need specific training i.e., librarian, statistician, and secretaries. Often a Sunday school will try to seek persons who already have experience in the area sought.

The support team has much to cope with. These workers, usually unpaid, dedicate their time, many times when they could be with family, all to do church work. Sometimes others have unrealistic expectations of these workers because it is often assumed that they have to continue holding the position.

The congregation can hinder the support team by allowing too much pressure to be upon the worker. A simple thing as having too many meetings may create a problem. Then too, some congregational leaders give additional assignments, often unrelated to that ministry. In addition, all day events on Saturdays and Sundays must be rethought.

Some church leaders plan a series of all day events. One must take into account that the support team has other things to complete. Many members have family members: children, wives or husbands or friends who seek their time. Church leaders' poorly planned decisions could easily be the reason for family neglect.

The Director of the Support Team

The Support Team needs a director. This director reports to the director of Christian education. The Support Team Director may train or provide training for all workers: specify the ministry and calendar to the Department of Christian Education, provide evaluation for the team, constant review assignments, provide assignments, or recommend team members to the desired ministry assignments. The director develops a commitment form and a job description. Specific training may be recommended or initiated by the ministry leader.

The Support Team should be trained. Training should include, but should not be limited to:

➢ Understanding Confidentiality

➢ How to Disciple Students

➢ The Flow Chart (Order of Command)

➢ The Do's and Don'ts for Each Age Group

➢ Spiritual Development for Each age Group

➢ Record Keeping

➢ Further study in the Word of God

➢ Preparation for the Assignment

➢ Job Description for the Interested Ministry

Ordering, Counting, and Distributing Sunday School Materials

A few weeks before Sunday church school material is ordered, the church school librarian or General Superintendent will contact each Sunday church school department superintendent to determine if the amount of materials needed has changed. The librarian or General Superintendent passes this information on to the Assistant General Superintendent for review. The superintendent orders the church school material a month and a half before the new quarter. This allows teachers one month to prepare quarterly lessons. Department superintendents should receive advance notice of the day and time they are to report to the church school office. Department superintendents distribute literature to their grade level(s). Teachers distribute literature to students.

Having a Support Team Ministry eliminates having workers feel "unwanted" or "used." Many times members of this ministry feel that they have the "left over" jobs. The Support Team Ministry is a very much needed team. Many of these team players are highly educated, but choose a different "type" of work. A ministry will allow workers to have more unity, feel more connected to the church, and perhaps will encourage them to do a better job. This team may receive assignments from the ministry leader. The ministry leader also provides supervision. The director only takes final action. The director of this ministry receives assignments from all church ministry leaders. The director reports to the director of Christian education.

Plans for the Support Team

Plans for the Support Team

Plans for the Support Team

Plans for the Support Team

Plans for the Support Team

CHAPTER SIX:
A MESSAGE TO
SUPERINTENDENTS

CHAPTER SIX:
A MESSAGE TO SUPERINTENDENTS

Superintendents can cause a Sunday school or church schools to flourish like a flower or die like a faded rose. Superintendents are the arm bearers for the Sunday school. The superintendent reports to the director of Christian education.

The superintendent must take his or her position seriously. The superintendent can encourage church members to attend the Sunday school or church school or could cause church members to neglect an opportunity to engage in Christian learning. The superintendent is responsible to teach the congregation the meaning of Sunday school and why one should attend. This means that sessions with the congregation might include the following discussion topics:

- [ ] School course offerings
- [ ] Why all ages should attend the church school
- [ ] Goals and objectives
- [ ] How the church school can help develop one spiritually
- [ ] The archaic view—"sending children" or "leaving children at home" no longer works
- [ ] No one is allowed to sit in the church pew during school hour, unless other assignments are given
- [ ] Teach Christians how to create an agenda for spiritual development. Include the Sunday school, Bible study, prayer life, Bible-reading, and ministry assignments
- [ ] Ask the congregation to suggest elective course-offerings
- [ ] Staffing needs
- [ ] Ways to improve the Sunday school or church school
- [ ] Review perhaps an alternate time for a second school day

The superintendent is a Christian who serves as a spiritual teacher between church and home. The Christian should be reminded that a superintendent and the church school are not the only responsible ones to teach Christian values. **Spiritual development at home is just as important as spiritual development at church and at Sunday or church school.**

The superintendent serves as resource person for the Sunday or church school.

Superintendents <u>should not</u> do the following:

⇨ Give too many assignments
⇨ Have unnecessary meetings
⇨ Require leaders, teachers, support staff, and students to use an entire day for volunteer work
⇨ Supervise children's church or youth church. These come under pastoral ministries
⇨ Shift responsibilities
⇨ Be over demanding
⇨ Make team members feel unwanted

Superintendents are also reminded of the school's schedule. A superintendent may have a devotional period for all classes. The devotional should be brief, no more than five minutes. Latecomers might never make it to a devotional period. An option is to have each teacher conduct his or her own devotions. The final wrap up, the conclusion, or dismissal period may be a group assembly or class benediction. Class devotions and end of school group assembly may work best.

The end of school assembly should include a brief wrap-up. Perhaps ask each teacher to schedule one student (a different one for each school day) to give a class overview in one minute or less. This session is not for a sermon or final instructions. This time is not provided for a meeting.

Superintendents have a great responsibility because the only time that students often meet to solely indulge in Biblical text may be during bible study. Sunday school classes usually meet for a longer period of time with a school-related focus. Bible studies may or may not have a school-related focus that requires a text other than the Bible.

Notes for the Superintendent

Notes for the Superintendent

Notes for the Superintendent

Notes for the Superintendent

Notes for the Superintendent

CHAPTER SEVEN:
THE FUTURE OF SUNDAY SCHOOLS OR CHURCH SCHOOLS AND TWO INTERVIEWS

CHAPTER SEVEN:
THE FUTURE OF SUNDAY SCHOOLS OR CHURCH SCHOOLS: INCLUDING TWO INTERVIEWS

The future of Sunday schools or church schools seems very promising. The church school is the foundational institution for spiritual learning. More and more church schools see a need to incorporate a structured school. Church schools in the new millennium are considering offering more electives for students. A point of caution is not to allow non-Christian based electives to replace the Christian curriculum. In addition to church school literature, some schools elect courses that require teachers to research or use present knowledge to teach students. The church school does need to consider ways for providing evaluations and promotions. Much thought should also be given to course titles.

The church school should consider more evaluations for church school leaders, teachers, support staff, and students. Church school leaders must visit and observe classes "in session." Leaders might consider contracting volunteers for shorter periods of time and make renewal optional for both, the teacher and the superintendent.

It is nice to report that most church schools seek staff that can get the job done.

Teacher training should not be held too frequently or for long periods of time. It is not the intent for teacher training to serve as a college classroom.

INTERVIEWS ABOUT THE CHURCH SCHOOL

Interviewed March, 2012 Mr. Eric Baskerville, M.S. Richmond, Virginia

Questions asked about the church school

☐ **What do you see as the primary purpose for the church school?**
To share the Good News of Christ and teach Christians how to implement God's rules and His Will in everyday life.

☐ **What five primary lessons should be taught in a church school?**

1. Who is Lord?
2. Who owns the Christian physical body?
3. What is the purpose of life?
4. Help students learn how to seek perfection
5. Help students how to fight between the "old" you and the "new" you

☐ **What five electives should be taught in a church school?**

- Stewardship
- Relationship with your children
- Relationship with your parents
- Parenting
- How to evangelize

☐ **Should the pastor play a role in the organization of the church school?**
Yes, the pastor should be a part of the school organization of the school because he is the main leader.

☐ **Why are young people turned away from the church or church school?**
There are reasons why people are turned away from church schools. I think people are turned away from church school because there are too many rules and too much authority. Also, some church leaders say one thing and do another.

□ **What can the church school do to encourage people to attend church and the church school?**
The church school must find a way to relate with people and find some type of common ground to build upon.

□ **What two problems do you see existing in the African American Sunday or church school?**
One problem that exists in the church school is the lack of men involved. In addition, the lack of in-depth study of the Word seems to be prevalent in some church schools.

□ **What two positive things do you see existing in the African American Sunday or church school?**
It is a place that anyone can go when they have nowhere else to go. It also provides hope: that our people will go above all trials and tribulations.

□ **What are your views about teachers in the African American church school?**
I think it's a two-headed coin. There are teachers who are passionate about their work, and take it as seriously as a job with a salary. Then there are others who show an attitude as if "Sunday school is the last thing on their minds."

□ **Should the Sunday school seek trained teachers? Why?**
I think sooner or later it might come to pass that students seeking more knowledge will need teachers who have skills to convey a higher learning to the uneducated.

□ **What kind of Sunday school would you like to see in the next ten years? Why?**
I would like the Sunday school in ten years to run like an academic school classroom. Teachers and students must be "serious" about spiritual learning.

Interviewed May, 2012

Mrs. Janice Oliver, M.A.; LPN
Richmond, Virginia

Questions asked about the church school

☐ **What do you see as the primary purpose for the church school?**

The primary purpose for church school is to educate each individual to have an understanding of Bible, learn about Jesus Christ, and apply the principles to daily living.

☐ **What five primary lessons should be taught in a church school?**

- The Creation (God)
- Birth of Jesus/Baptism
- Death of Jesus and His Resurrection
- Being a Christian
- The Unconditional Love of God in Christ

☐ **What five electives should be taught in a church school?**

- Christianity
- Discipleship
- Prayer
- Salvation
- Righteousness

☐ **Should the pastor play a role in the organization of the church school?**

Yes, the pastor's vision is important.

☐ **Why are young people turned away from the church or church school?**

They are turned away from church because some adults in church demonstrate a double standard. They are more interest in the enjoyment of the flesh.

□ **What can the church school do to encourage people to attend church and the church school?**

To witness to people about the Good News of Jesus Christ (how they can be saved) and discuss God's unconditional love. They can have a neighborhood educational, informative fair. Food and gospel music could be offered.

□ **What two problems do you see existing in the African American Sunday or church school?**

- Not trusting God (faith)
- Not having unconditional love for one another

□ **What two positive things do you see existing in the African American Sunday or church school?**

- Sinners being saved
- People are attending church and believing in a place where they can have hope

□ **What are your views about teachers in the African American church school?**

They should spend more time reading their Bible and preparing their lessons. Teachers are a vital component of African American churches.

□ **Should the Sunday school seek trained teachers? Why?**

Yes, because they already know about teaching, but they still have to be flexible enough to arrange these methods to teaching Sunday school.

□ **What kind of Sunday school would you like to see in the next ten years? Why?**

I would like to see a Sunday school that would be holistic, which would meet the needs of the whole person. It should center on reaching out to the community.

Interviewed June, 2012

Mr. William H. Ware, IV
Washington, D.C.

☐ **What do you see as the primary purpose for the church school?**

Teaching students how to apply God principles in daily life

☐ **What five primary lessons should be taught in a church school?**

- Who is Lord?
- Who owns the Christian physical body?
- How does one discover his or her purpose for life?
- Teach students how to seek spiritual perfection
- Help students how to fight between the "old" you and the "new" you

☐ **What five electives should be taught in a church school?**

- Stewardship
- Relationship with your children
- Relationship with your parents
- Parenting
- Evangelism

☐ **Should the pastor play a role in the organization of the church school?**

The pastor should oversee the school's organization and be familiar with the Sunday school curricula.

☐ **Why are young people turned away from the church or church school?**

I wouldn't contend that young people are "turned away," from church school; rather, they are turned off by it. The discrepancy between Christian teaching and real life is a barrier for immersion into church school. Some church schools may also be perceived as rigid with very little teaching application to modern reality.

☐ **What can the church school do to encourage people to attend church and the church school?**

The church must ensure that its' teaching are tailored to the audience it serves and to the community. Efforts must be made to pursue a process of change among students and to meet them where they are--intellectually, spiritually, and physically.

☐ **What two problems do you see existing in the African American Sunday or church school?**

Minimal male commitment to the church and a lack of trained educators.

☐ **What two positive things do you see existing in the African American Sunday or church school?**

The Sunday school usually accepts all students and makes an effort to impart the word of God.

☐ **What are your views about teachers in the African American church school?**

I think anytime individuals volunteer their time for the greater good and willing to learn teaching techniques are to be commended.

☐ **Should the Sunday school seek trained teachers? Why?**

Sunday schools should seek trained educators. They have the knowledge and skills to identify the needs of the students and tailor messages accordingly. They may relate better to students and provide techniques that are evidence-based for improving retention.

☐ **What kind of Sunday school would you like to see in the next ten years? Why?**

Within the next ten years I would like to witness the growth and transformation of church schools. Rather than their current state as auxiliary components of churches, I would hope for them to become mainstays; Sunday service(s) led by trained instructors passionate about the Word and teaching. These should be schools in which youth receive academic credit for participation and church member involvement is the rule rather than exception.

AFTERWORD 2010

Eric M. Baskerville, M.S.

This book, ***Don't Have A Messed Up Sunday School or Church School,*** is a **building block** for the Sunday school or church school. Sunday school or Church schools superintendents, teachers, support staff, pastors, and other leaders should read this book to replenish their school for the best in Christian education. Every big project starts with simple **blocks** which one adds to get where they desire to be. Dr. Oneal Sandidge has done exactly that. Every Sunday school or church school needs a solid **Christian block** as a foundation for things to build upon. Dr. Sandidge's research has provided ingredients for creating a **solid Christian block** for Sunday school administration. Dr. Sandidge educates us about the ABC's for creating a church school handbook.

A **block** has six sides. He has provided six chapters to build on. In addition, he has a seventh chapter, reminding us that a seventh element is needed to create a sturdy block. The seventh element is making sure that a person must carry out the building process. Dr. Oneal Sandidge looks at the seventh element as ***the Future of Sunday Schools or Church Schools,*** which indicates that someone must continue to lay the blocks.

A block must be solid or it is of no use at all. This book is solid because the substance and the content provide solid instruction. If you truly desire your Sunday school or church school to grow this manual should be at the top of your list to read.

Mr. Eric Maurice Baskerville, M.S. (Criminal Justice)

AFTERWORD 2012-Modern-Day Look

William H. Ware IV, M.S.

Our communities are in crisis. The War on Drugs combined with the prison industrial complex has spurred massive growth within the United States' correctional system. It is well known that the patrons of that system are disproportionately poor, minority, and particularly African American. The excessive incarceration of that population has resulted in deleterious consequences for families, communities, and our nation.

In this handbook, Dr. Oneal Sandidge provides a timely, step-by-step guide for church leaders to enhance the most fundamental institution of African American communities: the church and church schools. Dr. Sandidge has provided tools for the Sunday school that will encourage leaders to reach people who are in cells, out of cells, or persons who are simply lost. His concluding discussion with Mr. Eric Baskerville illuminates additional challenges to be faced by church leaders, specifically the lack of male involvement in churches and the difficulty of relating to our youth to encourage the life-long embodiment of God's teachings. These challenges will require innovative methods by church leaders that are built upon a foundation of research, intellect, and faith. Thankfully, this foundation has been laid by Dr. Oneal Sandidge.

Submitted 2012 by: William H. Ware IV, M.S.

(Criminology; Community Supervision Officer)

HIGHLIGHTS

This book is like no other book because it is the only known book to provide the ABC's for organizing or reorganizing the Sunday school or church school. The book is also loaded with suggestive forms to help any leader to construct his or her own forms for Sunday school or church school administration. This book reminds the prospective teacher, the current teacher, the VBS coordinator, training administrators, and the support team of their responsibilities.

Any church pastor, superintendent, church leader, professor of Christian education, or director of Christian education will find this book as a valuable tool in Christian education.

Index

P

pastors mission 6
promotional exercises 7
prospective teacher 6, 102, 105, 106, 107,
    149

R

records 7
retreats 7

S

school history 6
substitute teacher policies 7
superintendent 3, 4, 5, 6, 7, 103, 105, 106,
    137, 149
superintendents xxiii
support staff xxiii, xxiv, 6, 137

T

teachers xxiii, 6
theme 6

V

Vacation Bible School 6

Administration Recommended Resources

(Not responsible for Content)

Austin, S. (2006). *Crisis manual for Christian schools and youth workers: How to prepare for and handle tragedy.* Kansas City, MO: Beacon Hill Press of Kansas City.

Blazier, K. D. (1976). *Building an effective church school.* Valley Forge: Judson Press.

Church Educational Ministries. (1992). *More than Sunday school.* Wheaton: Evangelical Training Association.

Dinkins, C. (1983). *Manual for Sunday schools.* Nashville: Sunday School Publishing Board.

Dockrey, K. (1997). *Fun friend-making activities for adult groups.* Loveland, CO: Group Publishing.

Fergusson, E. (2010). *Church-school administration.* Charleston, SC: Nabu Press.

Fessenden, D. E. (2002). *Teaching with all your heart: Bringing curriculum & class to life.* Elgin, IL: Cook Communications Ministries.

Gangel, K. (2007). *Surviving toxic leaders: How to work for flawed people in churches, schools, and Christian organizations.* Eugene, OR: Wipf & Stock Publishers.

Gangel, K. O. (1975). *The effective Sunday school superintendent.* Wheaton: Scripture Press.

Gee, H. (2010). *Methods of church school administration.* Charleston, SC: Nabu Press.

Griggs, D. (2003). *Teaching today's teachers to teach.* Nashville: Abingdon Press.

Halverson, D. (1991). *How to train volunteer teachers.* Nashville: Abingdon Press.

Johnston, R. (1995). *Help! I'm a Sunday school teacher.* El Cajon, CA: Specialties, Inc.

Lankshear, D., & Hall, J. (2003). *Governing and managing church schools.* London: Church House Publishing.

LeFever, M. D. (2002). *Flowers from God: Thank-you notes for Sunday school teachers.* Elgin, IL: Cook Communications Ministries.

McGinley, S. (2000). *A moment with God for Sunday school teachers: Prayers for teachers or children.* Nashville: Dimensions for Living.

Melchert, C. F. (1998). *Wise teaching: Biblical wisdom and educational ministry.* Harrisburg, PA: Trinity Press International.

Ortberg, J. & Borton, R. (2001). *An ordinary day with Jesus: Experiencing the reality of God in your everyday life.* Barrington, IL: Willow Creek Resources.

Osmer, R. (1992). *Teaching for faith.* Louisville: Westminster Press.

Price, K. N. (1999). *Daily planning for today's classroom.* Albany, NY: Wadsworth Publishing Company.

Prosser, B., McCullar, M., & Qualls, C. (2008). *Building blocks for Sunday school growth.* Macon, GA: Smyth & Helwys Publishing, Inc.

Shalaway, L. (1998). *Learning to teach . . . Not just for beginners.* New York, NY: Scholastic Professional Books.

Spencer, R. (1994). *The work of the Sunday school superintendent.* Valley Forge: Judson Press.

Spohrer, J. (2003). *Serving your church nursery: Zondervan practical ministry guides.* Grand Rapids, MI: Zondervan.

Towns, E. (2002). *What every pastor should know about Sunday school.* Ventura, CA: Regal Books.

Youth Ministry Resources

Benjamin, I. S., & Watkins, R. (2009). *From Jay-Z to Jesus: Reaching and teaching young adults in the black church.* Valley Forge, PA: Judson Press.

Blazier, K. D. (1976). *Building an effective church school.* valley forge: Judson Press.

Burns, J., & DeVries, M. (2003). *Partnering with parents in youth ministry: The practical guide to today's family-based youth ministry.* Ventura, CA: Gospel Light.

Christie, L. J., & Holburn, K. S. (2005). *Best-ever games for youth ministry.* Loveland, CO: Group Publishing, Inc.

Chromey, R. (2009). *Youth ministry in small churches.* Loveland, CO: Group Publishing, Inc.

Church Educational Ministries. (1992). *More than Sunday school.* Wheaton: Evangelical Training Association.

Crabtree, J. (2011). *The complete new testament resource for youth workers, vol. 2.* Grand Rapids, MI: Zondervan/Youth Specialties.

DeVries, M. (2008). *Sustainable youth ministry: Why most youth ministry doesn't last and what your church can do about it.* United Kingdom: Inter-Varsity Books.

Dinkins, C. (1983). *Manual for Sunday schools.* Nashville: Sunday School Publishing Board.

Fields, D. (2002). *Your first two years in youth ministry: A personal and practical guide to starting right.* Grand Rapids, MI: Zondervan.

Fields, D., & Warren, R. (1998). *Purpose-driven youth ministry.* Grand Rapids, MI: Zondervan/Youth Specialties.

Gangel, K. O. (1975). *The effective Sunday school superintendent.* Wheaton: Scripture Press.

Group Magazine; Thom Schultz. (2006). *Best of try this one: The most popular ideas fro the #1 youth ministry resource.* Loveland, CO: Group Publishing.

Halverson, D. (1991). *How to train volunteer teachers.* Nashville: Abingdon Press.

Johnston, K. (2012). *99 thoughts about junior high ministry: Tips, tricks, & tidbits for working with young teenagers.* Group Simply Youth Ministries.

Jones, K. (2001). *Youth ministry that transform: A comprehensive analysis of the hopes, frustrations, and effectiveness of today's youth workers.* Grand Rapids, MI: Youth Specialties.

Jones, T. (2000). *Postmodern youth ministry: Exploring cultural shift, cultivating authentic community, crating holistic connections.* Grand Rapids, MI: Youth Specialties.

Kirk-Duggan, C., & Hall, M. (2011). *Wake up: Hip hop Christianity and black church.* Nashville, TN: Abingdon Press.

Kitwana, B. (2003). *The hip hop generation: Young blacks and the crisis in African American culture.* New York, NY: Basic Civitas Books.

Kunjufu, J. (2011). *What is the role of teens in your church.* Sauk Village, IL: African American Images.

Lawrence, R. (2007). *Jesus-centered youth ministry.* Loveland, CO: Group Publishing.

McCray, W. (1992). *Black young adults: How to reach them, what to teach them.* Chicago, IL: Black Light Fellowship.

McDowell, J., & Hostetler, B. (1996). *Handbook on counseling youth: A comprehensive guide for equipping youth workers, pastors, teachers, parents.* Nashville, TN: Thomas Nelson.

Melchert, C. F. (1998). *Wise teaching: Biblical wisdom and educational ministry.* Harrisburg, PA: Trinity Press International.

Middendorf, J. (2000). *Worship-centered youth ministry: A compass for guiding youth in God's story.* Kansas City, MO: BeaconHill Press of Kansas City.

Myers, W., Foster, C., & Kochman, T. (1990). *Black and white styles of youth ministry: Two congregations in America.* Bohemia, NY: Pilgrim Press.

Pahl, J. (2000). *Youth ministry in modern America: 1930 to the present.* Peabody, MA: Hendrickson Publishers.

Perkins, J., Elster, J., & Goode, W. W. (2008). *Playbook for Christian manhood: 12 key plays for black teen boys.* Valley Forge, PA: Judson Press.

Price, K. N. (1999). *Daily planning for today's classroom.* Albany, NY: Wadsworth Publishing Company.

Prosperi, W. (2006). *Girls' ministry 101: Ideas for retreats, small groups, and everyday life with teenage girls.* Grand Rapids, MI: Zondervan/Youth Specialties.

Reid, A. (2004). *Raising the bar: Ministry to youth in the new millennium.* Grand Rapids, MI: Kregel Academic & Professional.

Robbins, D. (2012). *Building a youth ministry that builds disciples: A small book about a big idea.* Grand Rapids, MI: Zondervan/Youth Specialties.

Sanders, N. (2005). *Bible crafts & more (ages 6-8) (HeartShaper resources-Elementary).* Cincinnati, OH: Standard Publishing.

Senter, M. (2001). *Four views of youth ministry and the church inclusive congregational, preparatory, missional, strategic.* Grand Rapids, MI: Youth Specialties.

Smith, E., Jackson, P., Kitwana, B., & Pollard, A. I. (2005). *The hip hop church: connecting with the movement shaping our culture.* United Kingdom: Inter-Varsity Press.

Watkins, R., Barr, J. J., & Harrison-Bryant, J. (2007). *The gospel remix: Reaching the hip hop generation.* Valley Forge, PA: Judson Press.

Yaconelli, M. (2006). *Contemplative youth ministry: Practicing the presence of Jesus.* Grand Rapids, MI: Zondervan/Youth Specialties.

Children's Resources

Beckwith, I. (2007). *The ultimate survival guide for children's ministry workers.* Ventura, CA: Regal Books.

Beckwith, I. (2010). *Formational children's ministry: Shaping children using story, ritual, and relationship.* Grand Rapids, MI: Baker Books.

Cartwright, T., & Keefer, M. (2005). *More than a movie: 20 fun specials for your children's ministry.* Loveland, CO: Group Publishing.

Christie, L. J., & Holburn, K. S. (2005). *Best-ever games for youth ministry.* Loveland, CO: Group Publishing, Inc.

Chromey, R. (2008). *Energizing children's ministry in the smaller church.* Cincinnati, OH: Standard Publishing.

Dollar, B., & Wideman, J. (2012). *I blew it! The biggest mistakes I've made in kids' ministry: And how you can avoid them.* Influence Resources.

Ervin, A. (2010). *Best practices for children's ministry: Leading from the heart.* Kansas City, MO: Beacon Hill Press of Kansas City.

Group Publishing. (2003). *Fun group games for children's ministry.* Loveland, CO: Group Publishing.

Group Publishing. (2012). *Seasonal specials for children's ministry: All-new ideas for 13 holidays.* Loveland, CO: Group Publishing.

Houser, T. (2008). *Building children's ministry: A practical guide.* Nashville, TN: Thomas Nelson.

Hudson, D. (2008). *Turbocharge! 100 simple secrets to successful children's ministry.* Loveland, CO: Group Publishing.

Jutila, C., Wideman, J., Yount, C., & Schultz, T. (2009). *Children's ministry that works! The basics and beyond.* Loveland, CO: Thom Schultz.

Lingo, S. (2003). *200+ activities for children's ministry.* Cincinnati, OH: Standard Publishing.

Maselli, C., Maselli, G., Butler, R., & Duke, R. (2008). *180 faith-charged games for children's ministry, elementary grades.* Greensboro, NC: Carson-Dellosa Christian Publishing.

Miller, S., & Staal, D. (2004). *Making your children's ministry the best hour of every kid's week.* Grand Rapids, MI: Zondervan.

Roehlkepartain, J. (2009). *Fidget Busters: 101 quick attention-getters for children's ministry.* Loveland, CO: Group Publishing, Inc.

ADULT RESOURCES

Arn, C., & Arn, W. (1999). *Catch the age wave: A handbook for effective ministry with senior adults.* Kansas City, MO: Beacon Hill Press of Kansas City.

Clark, D. (2000). *Feed all my sheep: A guide and curriculum for adults with developmental disabilities.* Louisville, KY: Geneva Press.

Davis, D. (2008). *Fresh ideas for women's ministry: Creative plans and programs that really work.* Nashville, TN: B & H Books.

Edwards, R. (2000). *Teaching adults: A guide for transformation teaching.* Nashville, TN: LifeWay Church Resources.

Ellison, R. (2006). *Spiritual food for Sunday school leaders: God's nourishmnet for effective service.* Montgomery, AL: Alabama Baptist Convention State Board of Missions.

Franck, D. (2007). *Reaching single adults: An essential guide for ministry.* Ada, MI: Baker Books.

Gallagher, D. (2006). *Senior adult ministry in the 21st centruy: Step-by-step strategies for reaching people over 50.* Eugene, OR: Wipf & Stock Publishers.

Halverson, D. (1997). *32 ways to become a great Sunday school teacher.* Nashville, TN: Abingdon Press.

Hendricks, H. (2003). *Teaching to change lives: Seven proven ways to make your teaching come alive.* Sisters, OR: Multnomah Publishers.

Houston, J., & Parker, M. (2011). *A vision for the aging church: Renewing ministry for and by seniors.* Inter-Varsity Press.

Hunt, J. (2005). *Ten marks of incredible teachers.* Las Cruces, NM: 2020 Vision.

Knippel, C. (2006). *How to minstry among older adults: As life's journey continues.* St. Louis, MO: Concordia Publishing House.

Parr, S., & Rainer, T. (2010). *Sunday school that really works: A strategy for connecting congregations and communities.* Grand Rapids, MI: Kregel Academic & Professional.

Rydberg, D. (1990). *Creative Bible studies for young adults.* Loveland, CO: Group Publishing, Inc.

Smith, C. (2009). *Souls in transition: the religious and spiritual lives of emerging adults.* New York, NY: Oxford University Press.

Toler, S., & Brecheisen, J. (2007). *The complete men's ministries kit: Everything you need to power up your program.* Kansas City, MO: Beacon Hill Press of Kansas City.

Touchton, D. (1995). *Leading adult learners: A handbook for all Christian groups.* Nashville, TN: Abingdon Press.

Feel Free to E-mail Dr. Sandidge for a church conference or preaching at your church. osandidge@hotmail.com.

BE BLESSED

DON'T HAVE A MESSED-UP SUNDAY SCHOOL OR CHURCH SCHOOL—

A BOOK TO HELP ORGANIZE YOUR SUNDAY SCHOOL OR CHURCH SCHOOL

Dr. Oneal Sandidge

This book is another book that every Christian educator must include in his or her library. The writer is not only an experienced Christian educator, professor, national lecturer, and work leader in Christian education, but he also presents a book to help you experience Sunday school or church school administration at its' best. This book is written from years of first hand experience. Every pastor, Director of Christian education, superintendent, church school leader and college/seminary professor must review this content.

ABOUT THE AUTHOR

Dr. Oneal Sandidge is an ordained minister, national lecturer, and workshop leader in Christian education. Dr. Sandidge is a member of Timothy Baptist Church in Amherst, Virginia where Rev. Scottie R.Craft is his pastor. He is the son of the late Wardie and Hattie Dawson Sandidge. Dr. Sandidge is married to Janice Oliver. He has two children: Ieke and Jermaine Sandidge; two godsons: Rev. Ronnie Clark and Eric Baskerville. Dr. Sandidge has served at a mega church in New York for two years, guiding 35 plus ministries and a wholesome Christian education. He was one of few full-time Directors of Christian Education in New York City. He has written eye-catching articles in Howard University Journal of Religious Thought, Sunday School Publishing Board, and United Methodist National Board for Christian Education to name a few. The national lecturer has assisted many pastors and congregations throughout the United States. He has provided training for many denominations, including United Methodist, Presbyterian USA, and Baptists conventions.

MEET THE EDUCATIONAL BACKGROUND OF

Dr. Oneal Sandidge, Ph.D.; D. Min.; M.R.E.; M.A.; B.A

- Post Doctorate Merrill's Fellow of Harvard
- A Virginia State University Graduate Writing Fellow
- PhD Scholar (Summa cum Laude) - Graduate in Education with a specialization in Adult and Higher Education Administration- Capella University, MN, MN
- Master's Online Certificate in Online Administration- Capella University, MN, MN
- Doctor of Ministry, Specialization in Christian Education. Dissertation on " Selecting Sunday School Literature in the African American Church" The third known breaking ground of research in the United States- Drew University, Madison, New Jersey
- Masters in Religious Studies/Masters in Education with a tri-specialization in History of the Black Church, and American Education and Christian Education—Columbia University, New York, New York (Honors)
- Masters in Religious Education- Howard University Divinity School, Washington, D.C.
- B.A. in Religion and Elementary Education-Grades 4-8, all subjects-Lynchburg College in Lynchburg, Virginia.
- Additional studies at Catholic University, Union Seminary in New York, Jewish Theological Seminary in New York, Virginia Union University, St. Paul's College, and University of Virginia

WORK EXPERIENCE OF
DR. ONEAL SANDIDGE

- Currently volunteers as interviewer for new potential students who seek admission to Harvard. He volunteers as an admissions interviewer for Virginia Alumni Chapter of Harvard College
- Former Dean of Religion, Arkansas Bible College- A fully accredited Institution- Higher Learning of Education
- Instructor Piedmont Community College, Charlottesville, Virginia
- Public School Teacher for 18 years
- An Online Professor- Liberty University-teaching more than 4,000 students in undergraduate and graduate religion and graduate educational research in the School of Education
- Dissertation Committee Member for awarding graduate students Ed.D./ Ph.D. degrees
- A Counselor for years
- A Director of Christian Education in a Mega Church

AWARDS FOR the Scholar,

Dr. Oneal Sandidge

- Dr. Sandidge is among the Hall of Fame Awards in Memphis Writers of Hall of Fame for Writers
- Recipient of the Lynchburg College Alumni Award posted in Lynchburg College Hall of Fame
- The Who's Who Among African Americans
- LABBE Los Angeles Book Expo Award
- Who's Who in American Universities and Colleges
- Listed among numerous Who's Who Awards
- Many other writing awards and essay contest awards
- Many church related and other unlisted awards
- Kappa Delta Pi Honor Society for Columbia University
- Who's Who In the World, 2001
- 1,000 Leaders of World Influence, 2000
- Outstanding People of the Twentieth Century, 2000, 2nd Ed.
- Who's Who International, 2000
- Dictionary of International Biographies, 2000
- Who's Who of the Southwest, 2000, 26th Ed.
- Who's Who in America, 2000, 54th Ed.
- Who's Who Among African-Americans, 1999-2000

Presentations

- Sandidge, O. (2005). History of the Black Church. Conference Presenter—Association for African American Historical Research and Preservation, Second Annual Conference—Seattle, WA
- Sandidge, O. (2008). How to teach learners to create an effective online discussion. Distance Learning Administration 2008 Conference. Jekyll Island, GA.
- Black History Month Presenter—Liberty University, 2007

MANY COURSES TAUGHT BY
DR. ONEAL SANDIDGE

- Public middle school English teacher
- All middle school subjects
- All elementary subjects
- Chair of Christian Education
- Advance Homiletics
- Parable of Jesus
- Graduate introductory courses in Christian Education
- Teaching Methods
- History of Christian Education
- Old Testament
- New Testament
- Evangelism
- Graduate Research
- Graduate Church
- Professor of Bible
- Professor of History of the Black Church
- Creative Teaching Methods
- The Books of John, Acts
- Apologetics

PUBLICATIONS

Sandidge, O. (2012). A book to change your life: The pastor's life, church life, and church leadership about ministry-A HOW TO DO MINISTRY BOOK. Florida: Xulon Press.

Sandidge, O. (2012). Don't have a messed-up Sunday school. Bloomington, IN: Author House.

Sandidge, O. (2009-2010). The African Sermon as a Teaching Tool. Journal of Religious Thought. DC: Howard University Press.

Sandidge, O. (2008). How to teach learners to create an effective online discussion. Distance Learning Administration 2008 Conference. Jekyll Island, GA.

Sandidge, O. (2007). Student perceptions of classroom discussion in an African American institution of higher learning. Ph.D. dissertation. Microfilm Abstracts.

September Eleven Maryland Voices. "The terrorist attack did not discriminate—poem." and "The color of life book—poem" "Set positive goals."

Sandidge, O. (2002). Teacher quit all the talking: The Christian Education Informer, 54(4). Nashville, TN: SSPB.

Sandidge, O. (2002). Can your students read scripture without knowing the vocabulary: The Christian Education Informer, 53(3)? Nashville, TN: SSPB.

Sandidge, O. (2001). Beyond the classroom. Nashville, TN: SSPB.

Sandidge, O. (2001). Strategies for the director of Christian education. Nashville, TN: SSPB.

Sandidge, O. (2001). Training African American church leaders in the new millennium. Nashville, TN: SSPB.

Sandidge, O. (2000). Assessing your students. The Christian Education Informer, 53(2). Nashville, TN: SSPB.

Sandidge, O. (2000). Back to basics: teaching teenagers at home and at school: The Christian Education Informer, 52(4). Nashville, TN: SSPB.

Sandidge, O. (2000). Twelve teaching tips for church educators: The Christian Education Informer, 52(4). Nashville, TN: SSPB.

Sandidge, O. (Dec. 1999- Jan. 2000). Teaching and the Holy Spirit: The Christian Education Informer, 52(3). Nashville, TN: SSPB.

Sandidge, O. (1999). A cake recipe to help pastors create a strong foundation for developing a Christian education program: The Christian Education Informer, 52(2). Nashville, TN: SSPB.

Sandidge, O. (1999). Students should be taught various pieces of the puzzle before leaving your class: The Christian Education Informer, 52(2). Nashville, TN: SSPB.

Sandidge, O. (1999). What do people need to know about Christian education in the church? : The Christian Education Informer, 52(2). Nashville, TN: SSPB.

Sandidge, O. (1998). Teacher -training in the African-American church. Nashville, TN: SSPB.

Sandidge, O. (1998). I'm stuck! Help me start a youth ministry in the African-American church. Nashville, TN: SSPB.

Sandidge, O. (Dec. 1995-Jan. 1996). Whosoever will come? Church School Today Leader. Nashville, TN: Abingdon Press.

Sandidge, O. (1995). Evaluating curriculum. Church School Today Leader. Nashville, TN: Abingdon Press.

Sandidge, O. (1992). The uniqueness of black preaching. The Journal of Religious Thought, 49(1). Washington DC: Howard University.

Sandidge, O. (1992). Tracing gospel roots with Professor Thomas Dorsey. Score Gospel Magazine, 3(1). Nashville, TN.

Sandidge, O. (January-February 1992). Black history. Virginia Education Association Journal

Sandidge, O. (1991). Black religious leaders–Conflict in unity. Journal of Black Scholars, 22(3). Madison, WI: University of Wisconsin.